# Pomo Indian Basketry

# Samuel Alfred Barrett

UNIVERSITY OF CALIFORNIA PUBLICATIONS

IN

AMERICAN ARCHAEOLOGY AND ETHNOLOGY

Vol. 7                                                           No. 3

# POMO INDIAN BASKETRY

BY

S. A. BARRETT

BERKELEY
THE UNIVERSITY PRESS
DECEMBER, 1908

**UNIVERSITY OF CALIFORNIA PUBLICATIONS**

IN

**AMERICAN ARCHAEOLOGY AND ETHNOLOGY**

VOL. 7                                               NO. 3

# POMO INDIAN BASKETRY.

BY

S. A. BARRETT.

## CONTENTS.

# INTRODUCTION.

Basketry, one of the most important and interesting of the textile arts, reached in California a very high state of perfection, connected probably with the fact that the California Indians led sedentary lives in a country abounding in a great variety of vegetation, upon which they depended chiefly for food and shelter, and which at the same time provided many tough pliable fibers which might be woven or coiled into articles of use. The California Indians taken together had a very great variety of materials, forms, methods of manipulation, and ornamentation of basketry. By certain of them, of course, only a limited number of materials, techniques, and designs were used but among others a greater variety was found.

Among no other California people was there so great a variety in basketry as among the Pomo, who occupied the greater part of Sonoma, Mendocino, and Lake counties, and vicinity. It is with the basketry of the Pomo, and particularly with its designs and other ornamentation, that the present paper has to deal. Information upon the general features of Pomo basketry, and to a certain extent upon their designs, was collected during some years of residence in the Pomo region, but it was not until 1904 that an attempt was made to systematically collect and verify all information possible concerning Pomo basketry and basket designs. This work was conducted as part of the investigations of the Ethnological and Archaeological Survey of California maintained by the Department of Anthropology of the University of California through the generosity of Mrs. Phoebe A. Hearst.

The general method pursued during the work was to question informants of three dialectic groups mentioned below, concerning the eight hundred and forty patterns shown on the photographs of three hundred and twenty-one Pomo baskets. Of this number seventy-one are photographs of baskets selected from the collections of the Museum of the Department of Anthropology of the University of California, one hundred and two are of a collection of baskets now the property of the Königliches Museum für Völkerkunde of Berlin, forty-one are from illustrations by Professor R. B. Dixon in his "Basket Designs of the Indians of Northern California,"[1] and the remainder are photographs of baskets seen among the Indians and from other miscellaneous sources. At the same time the Indians were also questioned concerning the designs on baskets they had, whenever this was possible. By securing good clear photographs of baskets it was found that informants had no difficulty in recognizing the designs, and that they were able to name them as easily as when they had the actual baskets before them. In this manner it was possible to obtain a greater range of information than otherwise could have been secured.

In all there are seven distinct and quite different dialects spoken by the Pomo, but of these only three, the Northern, Central, and Eastern, are to-day spoken by any considerable number of people. It is by the people of these three dialectic groups that basketry is most made and used at the present time, and it is chiefly from them that the information concerning basketry and basket designs was obtained.

With these people basketry in aboriginal times took the place of almost every sort of utensil, for the gathering, transportation, storage, grinding of vegetable products, cooking and serving foods, and for ceremonial and mortuary purposes. In short, from birth until death a Pomo used basketry for every possible purpose.

---

[1] Bull. Am. Mus. Nat. Hist., XVII, pt. 1, plates 27 to 36, 1902.

## MATERIALS.

### FIBERS AND RODS.

The materials used by the Pomo in basket making may be divided into two classes, those from which the basket proper is made and which are selected on account of their strength, and those materials which are used entirely for ornamentation and serve no essentially useful purpose. Almost all Pomo baskets, whether coiled or twined, are made upon a foundation of slender willow stems. The only other material so used is hazel, the slender stems of which are employed in the same manner as those of the willow. This material was used only in the northern part of the territory occupied by the Northern division of the Pomo and is probably attributable to contact with the Athapascans to the north who used hazel exclusively. About these stems, except in certain coarse open-work baskets, are coiled or twined pliable dressed fibers of several sorts, differing in color, so as to produce different designs, thus combining both the qualities of strength and ornamentation. To the second class of materials, those used entirely for purposes of ornamentation, belong the beads and bits of shell, and particularly the various feathers, which are found so frequently on Pomo baskets of the finer and ceremonial types.

The simplest kind of basket is that made entirely of slender willow or hazel stems, either peeled or unpeeled, these being used not only as the warp elements, but also being twined about as woof. Only the coarser open-work baskets, such for instance as fish and quail traps, coarse burden baskets, plate-form or hemispherical baskets used for sifting and as general receptacles, and seed-beaters, are made in this way. In these baskets the same method of manipulation, namely, plain twining, is found as in the brush fences built to snare or entrap deer, elk, rabbits, and quail, or in the brush wiers built across the streams for the trapping or spearing of fish. One type of seed-beater is also made in wickerwork. All baskets other than the coarse open-work ones above mentioned are made of two or more materials, the slender willow or hazel stems always being used as the foundation material.

There are several pliable dressed fibers which serve as wrapping material in coiling or as woof in twining. The most commonly used and most important of these materials is the root of the sedge, *Carex barbarae*. This plant, which grows about many of the springs and streams in the mountains but more particularly on the margins of lakes and ponds, produces a very long root stock the center of which is a tough woody fiber. This is gathered by means of a digging stick, and the outer covering having been removed is split into two long filaments, which are then, along with others, coiled into a roll and stored until needed. It is then moistened and dressed down to a size suitable for the kind of basket for which it is intended. The fine woody fibers of this root make it possible to dress these sewing elements down to a size hardly larger than that of fine thread, and it is from this material that almost all the very finest Pomo baskets are chiefly made. It is the material most used as the white background in all Pomo basketry, particularly the finer twined and coiled work. Among the Eastern Pomo who live in the vicinity of Clear lake where sedge and carex are abundant, another species of sedge called by them katsa'-kūhūm was mentioned as producing a similar white material. It would appear, however, that this plant is very little used, as almost none of the material was seen among any of the Pomo.

The material of next importance is the bulrush, *Scirpus maritimus*. This likewise is obtained from the root stock of the plant, which grows chiefly in the mud of the lake shore, usually at some distance out in the water. The round central fiber of this stock is when gathered of a light pink color, but is changed to a jet black or to various shades of brown by being buried in a mixture of the rich black mud of the lake shore with ashes. The degree of blackness varies according to the length of time the fibers are allowed to remain in this mixture, but the intention is always to produce a jet black material and it is not very often that the roots are removed before they have reached this stage. This material is used chiefly on the finer coiled baskets and on fine twined baskets, though it may of course find use on coarser ones of both types. When used, it is almost invariably this material that is employed to make the design itself, the white material being usually considered by the Indians as the background.

Next in importance to the bulrush as a basket material is redbud, *Cercis occidentalis,* from which two colors are obtained. The bark of this shrub is of a reddish brown color when gathered in the spring of the year. It, like the other materials, is split into long strips and made into coils which are stored until needed. Its chief use is as a red material, the outer surface of the outer bark being the part used in working out the design. There is also an inner bark, or more properly what is commonly called the sap wood, which produces a white material, which although not much used is occasionally found. The inner surface of the outer bark may also be brought into view instead of breaking this material off and inserting a new element of an ordinary white material. This may be considered a second white material obtained from the redbud. Also, upon soaking, the reddish outer surface of the bark changes to a dead black. These last two materials, however, are very rarely met with among the Pomo, though the first is frequently found among the Yuki to the north of the Pomo. The redbud when used as a red material is chiefly employed in designs on twined basketry, though it is also occasionally found upon coiled.

There are two other white materials which are in general use, one being the small inner fiber of the root of the willow, *Salix* sp. So far as has been found there seems to be no very great preference for any one of the several species of willow which abound in the Pomo country, the slender roots which grow out into the water of lakes and streams being taken from all. Some maintain that the best fiber is obtained from the root of the same willow the stems of which are used as the foundation material. This material is sometimes used in the finer coiled baskets, but is chiefly used in twined or in coarse coiled work. It must, however, be counted as one of the materials more rarely used and is said by the Indians themselves to be much inferior to sedge or pine root on account of its brittleness when dry.

The other white material found in use among the Pomo of these three divisions, is the root of what is commonly called the digger pine, *Pinus sabiniana.* Various sized roots of this pine are dug, and after being heated in hot ashes or by holding them directly over the fire, are split into long coarse fibers, which are coiled and stored for use. By wetting, these, like the other materials, become pliable and may be split into fibers of almost any desired size. They find use almost exclusively in the making of large twined baskets, and while not so much used as the sedge are quite often found. In addition to these two white materials there is still another obtained probably from the root of the juniper, *Juniperus occidentalis.* This, however, appears to be very little used. Its preparation and uses are the same as those of the digger pine.

There is a second black material, the root fiber of the bracken, *Pteridium aquilinum.* Within the root of the bracken there are several flat fibers sometimes reaching a width of three-eighths of an inch. These are when gathered a light brown in color, and are usually made into coils and stored until needed, though they may be treated to blacken them immediately. This is done by boiling them for a short time, and here again the length of time they are treated governs the blackness of the fiber, so that it sometimes happens that baskets are found with this fiber in various shades of brown instead of black. It is, like the bulrush, used entirely as a material in which to work basket designs on a background of various white materials, and finds use chiefly in the finer twined baskets or in coarser coiled work. It is also noticeable that this material is, at the present time at least, more frequently used upon the immediate coast than in the interior valleys, though it is quite frequently found there also.

The above mentioned constitute the materials used for making Pomo baskets in general. There are, however, two other materials which find special uses in basketry. One is the sap wood of the grape, *Vitis californica.* The sap wood of the grape is a very tough pliable fiber and found general use among the Pomo as a binding material, being used for everything where a twisted string or rope of strands of twisted fiber was not absolutely demanded. It thus found use to a certain extent in the making of brush fences for the capture of various kinds of game, it was used to bind rafters, stringers, and posts in the making of the large ceremonial earth lodges, and in all other cases where a strong pliable binding material was required. In connection with basketry it finds use in binding the hoop which is always placed about the opening of a conical burden basket or about the upper opening of a mortar or milling basket, and occasionally about the opening of a basket of the openwork sifter type.

A second specialized material is the tule, *Scirpus*. The long stems of two species are used, one, *Scirpus lacustris* var. *occidentalis,* with a circular cross section; the other, *Scirpus robustus,* with triangular cross section. As might be expected, these materials were not found throughout the Pomo region, but were chiefly confined to the vicinity of lakes and ponds, and it was only in such regions as the vicinity of Clear lake that they were used to any extent. They were employed for making certain plain-twined baskets, but from the nature of the material no fine work could be done with them. Their chief use was in the vicinity of Clear lake, where, in addition to baskets, boats were made from the first mentioned, and mats and house thatch from the second.

In addition to the slender willow stems above mentioned, used in almost all cases as foundation material, and the root, used as a weft or sewing material, the willow provides one other material used in connection with basketry, namely: the heavy hoop bound about the opening in the conical burden basket, and about the upper opening in the mortar or milling basket, as also about the opening of some baskets of the openwork sifter type.

### FIBER MATERIALS.

| English | Northern | Central | Eastern |
|---|---|---|---|
| Sedge (*Carex barbarae*) | kŭhŭ′m | kŭhŭ′m | kŭhŭ′m |
| Sedge (*Carex* sp.) | kadī′ kŭhŭm | | katsa′-kŭhŭm |
| Bulrush (*Scirpus maritimus*) | tsīwi′c | tsīwi′c | tsīwi′c |
| Redbud (*Cercis occidentalis*) | mille | kala′ia | dīsa′i |
| Redbud (inner bark) | millē-to′i | kala′ia-katō | dīsai-tō′ts, tacī′ma |
| Digger pine (*Pinus sabiniana*) | kale′-ce | kale′-ce | kale′-ce |
| Juniper (*Juniperus occidentalis*) | | catco′m | cate′p |
| Willow root (*Salix*) | kala′l-yem, ma-yem | ma′-ce | gaiī′-ce |

| English | Northern | Central | Eastern |
|---|---|---|---|
| Bracken | bi's-yem | mao'dŏ-kit | lī'bītsits |
| (*Pteridium aquilinum*) | | | |
| Grape | cīyi'n | ctin | ctīn |
| (*Vitis californica*) | | | |
| Tule² | badjŏ' | batcŏ' | bag'ŏ' |
| (*Scirpus lacustris* var. | | | |
| occidentalis) | | | |
| Tule² | gīca'l | | gūca'l |
| (*Scirpus robustus*) | | | |
| Willow stem | kala'l, bam | kala'l | tsū'baha |
| Willow hoop | dakŏ' | dako' | dakŏ' |
| Hazel | batī | | |
| (*Corylus rostrata* var. | | | |
| californica) | | | |

### FEATHER AND SHELL MATERIALS.

One of the most noticeable and characteristic features of Pomo basketry, and the feature which did much to bring it into great favor with collectors, is feather decoration. Certain other peoples, the Yuki, the southern Wintun and perhaps others in northern California, and the Yokuts and Shoshonean tribes and perhaps others in south central California, used feathers to a very limited extent on certain specialized forms of baskets, but no other California people appear to have used feathers to entirely cover their baskets as was done by the Pomo. In recent years the Yuki, the southern Wintun, the Yukian Wappo and the portion of the Moquelumnan stock living north of San Francisco bay, all of whom were immediate neighbors of the Pomo, have made some attempt at elaborate feather decoration but so far as can be learned no such decoration was practiced by them in aboriginal times, and very few if any good specimens of elaborately decorated baskets are now made by them. The Pomo, on the other hand, have so far perfected this form of decoration that they are able to cover their baskets completely with feathers, and good basket makers can so place them that the surface of the basket has almost the smoothness of the breast of a bird itself. Such feathered baskets are shown in pl. 21, figs. 1, 2, 4, 5. Some of the older basket makers maintain that in aboriginal times they used only the feathers from the top of the

---

² The first of these species of tule has a stem with circular cross-section, while the stem of the second has a triangular cross-section.

head and from the throat of the redheaded woodpecker, those from the head of the mallard duck, and the top-knot of the quail. Others however state that the feathers of several other birds were also used, and at the present time feathers from the following species are employed.

From the bright red crest of the redheaded woodpecker, *Melanerpes formacivorus,* small feathers are obtained which are used in various ways in basketry, chiefly in the making of the red feathered basket which has become known to the whites as the "sun basket," though it is not so called by the Indians themselves. In addition to this basket, the surface of which is entirely covered with red feathers from the head of the woodpecker, various other baskets are decorated with these and other feathers. Some are covered completely while others are covered only partially as is shown in pl. 19, fig. 4, where the red feathers of the woodpecker are scattered at intervals over the surface of this boat-shaped basket except where the pattern itself appears. Often they are used with other feathers in such a manner that very effective patterns like those made in basket fibers are worked out. No very elaborate patterns however are attempted in feathers. Upon the throat of this same bird there is a patch of feathers of lemon color which are also used in basket decoration.

Next in importance to the red feathers from the woodpecker are the jet black plumes from the top-knot of the California valley quail, *Lophortyx californicus.* These, while they are never used as the complete covering of a basket, are much employed to ornament the borders of feathered baskets as is shown in pl. 21, fig. 2, or to scatter over the surface among other feathers. They are also often used even upon the finer twined baskets without other feathers as is shown in pl. 16, fig. 6. The plume of the male is much longer and is more highly prized than that of the female, but both are used. Occasionally also, though it occurs so rarely that this can hardly be counted as one of the regular basket materials, the long slender black plume of the California mountain quail, *Oreortyx pictus,* is used in the same manner as the shorter club-shaped plume of the valley quail.

The green head of the mallard duck, *Anas boschas,* also provides an important material for ornamenting baskets. Baskets are entirely covered with these green feathers in the same manner as with the red feathers of the woodpecker, and by analogy this basket has become known to the whites as the "moon basket," although here again without any valid reason, as the Indians do not call it by any such name.

Another bird, the feathers of which are considerably used, is the meadowlark, *Sturnella magna.* The yellow feathers from the breast of this bird are at present frequently used.

The feathers of the bluebird, *Sialia,* are occasionally used, as are also the feathers of the California jay, *Cyanocitta californica.*

The oriole, *Icterus bullocki,* provides feathers of an orange color which are used with the lighter yellow feathers of the meadowlark.

The feathers of the varied thrush, *Ixoreus naevius,* commonly called the mountain robin, which has a dark brown breast, are often used at the present time and produce a very pleasing effect.

The feathers of the ordinary robin redbreast, *Merula migratoria,* are used, at least by some basket makers, to a very limited extent.

The red feathers from the shoulder patches of the red-winged blackbird, *Agelaius phoeniceus,* are sometimes employed in basketry. The black feathers of this bird are more rarely used.

One other kind of feather which has upon one or two occasions been noticed in use is that from the black head of the brant, *Branta canadensis.*

All these feathers except the quail plume are used only upon coiled baskets and among these chiefly upon baskets of three-rod foundation.

Together with the feather ornamentation goes the ornamentation with shell and magnesite beads, and with variously shaped bits of iridescent abalone shell. The disk beads of clam-shell, *Saxidomus nuttallii,* are used about the opening of a basket as a border, being placed in a continuous line, as is shown in pl. 21, figs. 5, 6, or in groups of usually three or four beads at three or four equidistant points about the opening, as is shown in pl. 19, fig. 4. They are also made into ornamental handles, such as those shown on the baskets in pl. 21, by which the finer, particularly feathered, baskets are hung, and are also used for making pendants which are suspended from the border of the opening or from various points over the surface of the basket, as is shown in pl. 21, fig. 2. The red magnesite disks are but rarely found on baskets, but when used are employed in the same manner as the white clam-shell beads. Variously shaped, usually triangular, bits of iridescent abalone shell are placed at the ends of the pendant strings of beads as is shown in pl. 21, figs. 1, 2, and pl. 19, fig. 5. For the fastening of these beads and abalone pendants, as also for the making of the bead handles and for the fastening of the beads about the border of the basket, native string of milk-weed or other native fiber was used in aboriginal times. How-ever in some cases where beads are attached singly at intervals over the surface of a basket, as is shown in the large lattice-twined storage basket in pl. 17, fig. 2, they are fastened with the sewing or twining fiber itself. Beads, like feathers, are rarely used on twined basketry, and their chief use is together with feathers on coiled baskets of three-rod foundation, though they are often used without feathers upon both three-rod and single-rod foundation baskets.

### FEATHER AND SHELL MATERIALS.

| English | Northern | Central | Eastern |
|---|---|---|---|
| Redheaded woodpecker (*Melanerpes formacivorus*) | kata'tc | kata'k | kara'tc |
| Mallard (*Anas boschas*) | kaia'n | kaia'n | kaia'n |
| Quail, valley (*Lophortyx californicus*) | caka'ka | caka'ka | cag'a'x |
| Quail, mountain (*Oreortyx pictus*) | kohō'ī | kohō'ī | |
| Lark (*Sturnella magna*) | djicī'l | cīl | gŭcī'lī |
| Oriole (*Icterus bullocki*) | ka'iyōyŭ | kaiyōī | tsaga'tsagaŭ |
| Red-winged blackbird (*Agelaius phoeniceus*) | bilī'ya | tsilī' | tsŭ'Lī |
| California Jay (*Cyanocitta californica*) | tsai | tsai | tsai |
| Bluebird (*Sialia*[8]) | kalītcō'tcō | ta'-tsakat | kacī'ltsīya |

[8] Two species of bluebird, the Western bluebird, *Sialia mexicana*, and the Mountain bluebird, *Sialia arctica*, are found in this region.

| English | Northern | Central | Eastern |
|---|---|---|---|
| Robin | tsĭto'ktok | tsatŏ'tŏ | tsitŏ'tŏ |
| *(Merula migratoria)* | | | |
| Varied thrush or mountain | | | |
|   robin | sĭ'wa | sĭ'wa | sĭ'wa |
| *(Ixoreus naevius)* | | | |
| Yellowhammer or red- | | | |
|   shafted flicker | batsĭ'ya | katsĭ'ya | tĭya'l |
| *(Colaptes cafer)* | | | |
| Brant | | | |
| *(Branta canadensis)* | | | |
| Shell beads | kn'ia | talē'ya | ca'tanĭ |
| *(Saxidomus nuttallii)* | | | |
| Magnesite beads | po | po | pol |
| Abalone shell | te'm-gata | wĭl | |
| *(Haliotis)* | | | |

## TECHNIQUE.

### TWINING.

In the matter of technique Pomo basketry shows great variety. The Pomo probably possessed a greater number of weaves than any other people in California. They had one weave, lattice twining, possessed by no other people, so far as is now known, except the Yukian Huchnom, whose small territory joined that of the Pomo on the north and who, while entirely distinct in language, are in culture very similar to the Pomo. Excluding from consideration temporarily the special weaves used for finishing borders of baskets, the Pomo have five distinct forms of twining:[4] plain-twined, diagonal-twined, lattice-twined, three-strand-twined, and three-strand-braided. Of these twined weaves the first three are in common use, while the two three-strand weaves are chiefly used in starting the bottoms of baskets and in finishing the borders. Three-strand twining is sometimes used throughout an entire basket such as is shown in pl. 25, fig. 6. Three-strand braiding is almost never so used.

The plain-twined method of weaving is on the whole the most used. It is employed for all forms of twined basketry, including

---

[4] The terms used in connection with weaves in the present paper are those so well and completely described and defined in Professor Otis T. Mason's "Aboriginal American Basketry," Ann. Rep. Smith. Inst., pp. 221-278, 1902.

some which are never made in other twined weaves. Basketry among the Pomo, as among almost all aboriginal peoples, is essentially a woman's art, and all of the coiled and practically all twined baskets are made by the women. The men employ only the plain twined and the three-strand twined weaves. The first they use in making fish traps of five forms, shown in pl. 27, figs. 2-6; quail traps, pl. 28, fig. 3; and occasionally coarse openwork burden and storage baskets, pl. 26, though the burden baskets are sometimes also made by the women. Three-strand twined weaving is only used occasionally in an openwork burden or a hemispherical openwork basket of the sifter type, such as is shown in pl. 25, fig. 6. Diagonal and lattice twining are also much used in the making of cooking baskets, like those shown in pl. 16, fig. 3, and pl. 17, fig. 4; plate-form baskets used for winnowing, parching, etc., like those shown in pl. 23, figs. 1, 2; and large tightly woven storage baskets, like that shown in pl. 17, fig. 2. Lattice twining also finds frequent use in the making of hemispherical or plate-form openwork baskets (pl. 25, fig. 3), used as sieves and general utensils. On the other hand this weave is never used in making conical burden baskets, while diagonal twining is very frequently so used (pl. 22, figs. 1-5).

A special weave related to lattice twining is employed in the making of one form of basket, the cradle. As in lattice twining, there are rigid elements running both vertically and horizontally; and like it also, the pliable weaving elements are two in number. The single horizontal rigid element is in all respects the same as that used in lattice twining except that in some cases at least it is semicircular instead of circular in cross-section. The two pliable weaving elements are, however, usually some form of string, though the ordinary weaving fibers are sometimes used. In the case of lattice twining these pliable elements are manipulated as in plain twining, except that in the twining they include not only the vertical elements but also the horizontal one. In the special weave used in cradles, however, these two pliable elements are woven together in a very intricate fashion, the details of which may be seen in pl. 15, fig. 7.

In the exact manipulation of the elements used in the various kinds of weaving there are certain differences to be noted. All tightly woven baskets are made with a downward turn[5] of the woof strands and nearly all openwork baskets are made with an upward turn of these elements.

Since the men make no tightly woven baskets, and the women make very few openwork baskets, it may be said in general terms that the upward turning of the woof is employed by men and the downward by women.[6] Since the women use plain twining, diagonal twining, lattice twining, three-strand twining, and three-strand braiding, all these are made with the downward turn of the elements. The men use only plain twining and three-strand twining and these, therefore, are the only ones which are made with an upward turn of the woof strands. Up-turned plain twining is found only in openwork burden baskets, fish traps, and flat baskets of the sifter type, and three-strand twining only in burden baskets and sifters, both of which, however, are rarely so made. No openwork diagonal-twined baskets are found, and lattice-twined openwork baskets are made only by women, and have the downward turn of the woof strands. The special weave used in making the cradle and illustrated in pl. 15, fig. 7, above referred to, is another technique employed by the men.

Both three-strand twining and three-strand braiding are always so woven that two of the strands appear on the outside and one on the inside of the basket. In almost all cases both these are so woven that each strand passes over two warp sticks on the outside of the basket, and over one warp stick on the inside. Exceptions occur only in the three-strand weaving immediately about the starting knots upon the bottoms of baskets. In such cases the number of warp sticks included in each turn may

---

[5] By downward turn is meant twining which progresses in such a manner that when it is viewed from the end and in the direction toward which it progresses, the strands revolve about each other in a clockwise direction. Thus, when the outer surface of the basket is viewed, each woof strand, as it emerges from behind a warp stick takes a downward turn and passes behind a succeeding warp stick on the lower side of the line of twined woof strands. By an upward turn is meant, of course, the opposite of downward turn, and in this method of weaving the woof strands appear, when the outer surface of the basket is viewed, to pass from the lower side of the line of twining upward, and to disappear behind the warp sticks on the upper side of the line.

[6] The only exception to the latter part of this statement is in the case of openwork burden and openwork flat baskets of the sifter type, which are made by both men and women, though chiefly by men.

be doubled, thus making each woof strand pass over four stems outside and over two stems inside the basket. In the ordinary three-strand twining and three-strand braiding the inner surface of the basket presents the same appearance as a basket of plain twined weave, while in cases where the woof strands pass over twice the usual number of warp sticks the appearance of the inside is that of diagonal twining. The outer surface in the latter case appears quite different from the surface of ordinary three-strand weaving. The woof strands appear to overlap each other much more, by reason of their passing over four instead of two warp sticks, and therefore covering a greater segment of the circle of twining. Further, as these methods of twining are only used near the starting knots of baskets, these circles are naturally quite small, which further accentuates the overlapping appearance of both these weaves with double warp. These two weaves appear to be used only upon baskets made by women and in all cases have a downward turn of the weaving elements.

As before stated, three-strand twining and three-strand braiding are both used chiefly as border finishes and in the bottoms of baskets. The ordinary form only of each of these two weaves is used as border finish, and it is much more commonly used upon the bottoms of baskets than is the one where the woof strands include four warp sticks. However, none of the three-strand weaves are in very common use, even as border finish or upon the bottoms of baskets. Probably not more than half of the tightly woven twined baskets have borders or bottoms in which one of the three-strand weaves appears. Among openwork baskets on the other hand the bottoms have no special weaves. The borders are of quite a different nature, being in almost all cases of the warp-turned-down order, with now and then a basket of the sifter type possessing a border bound with a hoop.

## TWINING.

| English | Northern Pomo | Central Pomo | Eastern Pomo |
|---------|---------------|--------------|--------------|
| Twining | djama' | tcama'ū, cee't | kǐ'cki |
| Plain twined | bam-tū'c | bam-tū'c | xai-xa'lǐ, bam-tū'c |
| Diagonal twined | cūse't | bam-sa'i | cūsa's |
| Lattice twined | t!ǐ' | haině'dū | tcǐga', tū'ga |
| Three strand tw. | cǐtaǐ'n | cwi'tki | cūwǐ'ri |
| Three strand br. | cǐtaǐ'n | cwi'tki | cūwǐ'ri |
| Wickerwork | djama'? | itǐ't? | dūka'l |

### Starting Knots.

The Pomo have four general methods of starting the foundations of twined baskets: warp sticks crossed in pairs, warp sticks crossed in threes, warp sticks crossed in fours, and sets of warp sticks bound separately with plain twining and the sets crossed. All the knots formed by these various methods, as well as those used in making coiled baskets, are called by the Northern Pomo būm or sīli', by the Central Pomo būm or ptsat, and by the Eastern Pomo sīli'x.

Of these various methods, the one in which the warp sticks are crossed in pairs is the one most frequently employed. All plain-twined, openwork baskets, except such long cylindrical fish traps as have no bottoms made of the regular warp sticks used in the sides, and most of the openwork baskets of other weaves are made with this knot. The greater number of closely woven twined baskets are also made with this knot.

There are three methods of manipulation of this particular knot which have thus far been observed. The simplest of these is the one shown in pl. 15, fig. 3, in which the two pairs of warp sticks are crossed without being bound together or wrapped in any way except as they are held together by the regular twining of the weft elements. In a second method the two pairs of sticks are simply crossed and wrapped so that the weft elements pass diagonally across the whole set and through the angles formed by the two pairs of sticks, as in the center of pl. 15, fig. 1. Sometimes also the wrapping fiber passes between the sticks of each pair, thus forming a cross whose arms are parallel to the pairs of sticks, as in pl. 15, fig. 2. The most complicated method, the one most commonly found in use on tightly twined baskets, is the one in which part of the wrapping passes diagonally across through the angles formed by the pairs of sticks, and another part of the wrapping goes across one of the pairs of sticks and parallel to the other pair, as shown in pl. 15, fig. 1. This makes a small square about the diagonal cross of wrapping fiber. It is by this last wrapping that the points of newly inserted sticks are bound, thus making a radial bottom upon which the twining is commenced.

The foundation in which the warp sticks are in sets of three (pl. 15, fig. 6) has so far been found in but few baskets. The wrapping in this case is all done on lines parallel to the one set of sticks and at right angles to the other, thus forming a square of the binding material and holding the sticks of each set closely together and making a very tightly drawn cross of the two sets. In at least some instances of this binding, most of the first few rounds of twining on the bottom of the baskets are of diagonal-twined weave, the remainder of the basket being in lattice twining. In the first round of diagonal twining on such baskets two of the three crossed sticks are bound together between two woof elements, the third, together with a newly inserted warp stick, being included in the next turn of the two-woof strands. This newly inserted warp stick, of course, occupies the angle between the two sets of three warp sticks. The next turn of the woof strands therefore includes two of the other set of three warp sticks, and the next turn again includes the remaining one of the three with another newly inserted warp stick, and so on until the whole round is completed. In some cases the first round of weaving is plain twining, but this is followed by the diagonal twining as above described. Warp sticks crossed in threes may also be used without the above mentioned binding, in which case the twining proceeds as in the case of the warp sticks crossed in pairs shown in pl. 15, fig. 3.

The third method of making the foundation for twined baskets is by means of warp sticks crossed in fours. These sets of warp sticks may be bound at right angles to each other by fibers passing diagonally over the warp sticks and through the angles of the cross formed by these sticks. These fibers may be passed through one or both sets of diagonally opposed angles. The pairs of each four are then bound together with continuous twining fibers, thus serving to further bind the whole eight sticks more securely together. This produces such a foundation as is shown in pl. 15, fig. 5. In addition to this method there is usually another binding in which a single fiber passes at right angles to one set of fours and through the successive spaces between the other set of fours, the rods of which are of course at right angles to the first set and parallel to the direction of this fiber itself. This gives a binding of three strands of fiber which pass entirely around one set of the fours and parallel to the other set. The appearance is that of very long stitches. As this fiber comes from between the last two of the sticks of the one set of four it passes over the side of the outer one and down on the outside of this set. This may complete the binding, or the same fiber may then be passed in a similar manner between the successive sticks of the other four and thus run at right angles to its former course. Still further binding is sometimes done by passing fibers diagonally across from a pair of one set of fours to the adjacent pair of the other, thus enclosing the two pairs in the same binding. When completed this produces a square the sides of which are at angles of forty-five degrees to the warp sticks. This sort of starting knot may be further complicated by the addition outside of this of another square of binding fiber the sides of which are at right angles to one and parallel to the other set of warp sticks, thus forming angles of forty-five degrees with the sides of the last mentioned square. This same framing of squares about one another while perfectly possible is rarely found in the other knots.

Another method of laying these foundations for twining, related to that just described, is by the use of four sticks in two pairs on the outside of the basket, and a single pair on the inside, as is shown in pl. 15, fig. 4. The outer four sticks are so bound that they appear as separate pairs, while the whole six are bound together with a cross of fibers, and this enclosed in a square of fibers as was described in speaking of the most elaborate of the methods of binding the foundation made of warp sticks crossing in pairs.

As in the case of warp sticks crossed in pairs (pl. 15, fig. 3), the twining upon a foundation of warp sticks crossed in fours may proceed directly without any special binding, though this is rarely found.

The method in which warp sticks are bound together by plain twining and two of these sets of warp sticks are then crossed and bound together with plain or diagonal twining is shown in pl. 15, fig. 9. Sets of four and sets of five of these warp sticks are employed in this manner, though both are of very rare occurrence.  Thus far they have been found in use only upon open-work baskets of lattice-twined weave.

One other method of starting is employed in making the specialized form of sifting basket shown in pl. 23, fig. 6.  Here a short stick about half an inch in diameter is split into several small rods or welts at one end, the other end being left entire. The woof fibers are then twined about these small rods or splints in the same manner as though they were ordinary warp sticks.

### Border Finishes.

In twined basketry the Pomo have a number of methods of finishing borders all of which weaves are called by the Northern Pomo tsawa′m, by the Central Pomo mto′t and tsawa′m and by the Eastern Pomo tsawa′mk.  In fact almost all twined baskets have some kind of a border finish which is quite different from the weave of the body of the basket.  Now and then, however, a globose twined cooking basket is found which has no special border finish weave, and quite a number of plate-form baskets lack any finishing weave about their borders.  One of the characteristic features of Pomo basketry is that in almost all cases, whether the borders are finished with a special weave or not, the ends of the warp sticks are cut off so that they project quite perceptibly above the last course of twining.  In most other types of basketry, such as that of the Yurok, Karok and Hupa of Northwestern California these warp sticks are cut off just even with the last course of twining.

In the closely woven baskets of the various twined weaves several of these border finishes are found, but no one appears to be confined to baskets of any particular weave.  In some cases the change of weave at the border is quite a simple one.  For instance, baskets of lattice twining or diagonal twining are frequently found with simply a few rows of plain twining at the border.  In other lattice-twined or diagonal-twined baskets the borders may be finished with a few rows of plain twining and above these one or two rows of three-strand twining or three-strand braiding, and over this again there may be one or more rows of plain twining.  Either three-strand twining or three-strand braiding may also be used alone as a border finish.

Diagonal twining is occasionally found as a border finish of lattice or plain twined baskets. Lattice twining on the other hand is almost never found alone as a border finish.

A set of very commonly occurring weaves used as border finish, while essentially the same as plain twining, differs from it in that the twining is upon dual or multiple warp as shown in pl. 15, fig. 8. In these multiple warp weaves the weft elements may include two, three, or four warp sticks about which the twining proceeds in exactly the same manner as though they were single warp sticks instead of groups. In this manner the effect of a set of square or rectangular blocks is produced in the space immediately at the rim of the basket. These blocks are sometimes all of the same color, but usually they are alternately red and white, or black and white, thus producing a row of rectangular figures commonly called by the Pomo here treated, "finishing design." This weave is found occasionally about the border of a cooking or a plate-form basket, and may be at the very rim of the basket or may have above it one or more rows of one of the common weaves. It appears most frequently in those baskets which are bound with hoops.

The baskets bound with hoops are, conical burden baskets, mortar baskets, and occasionally shallow openwork baskets of the sifter type; the last having hoops only when they are of the lattice-twined weave. The hoop is bound on by a process of sewing the same as is used in coiled basketry, the spiral made by the sewing fiber including the uppermost row or two of twining in the basket itself and passing entirely around the hoop. It is so closely bound about the hoop in most cases as to completely hide it. Illustrations of this hoop binding are seen in the plate of burden baskets (pl. 22). The appearance of the inner part of such a hooped rim is shown in the mortar basket illustrated in pl. 23, fig. 4. Just below this hoop in almost all burden baskets there is a row of the above mentioned small squares of plain-twined weave including two, three, or four warp sticks. This row may be immediately below the hoop or it may be separated from it by one or more rows of plain or diagonal twining. It very rarely happens that a basket bound about the rim with such a hoop has not immediately below it a few rows of some weave which is different from that of the remainder of the basket.

Openwork twined baskets have border finishes of two general types. The simplest of these is what may be termed the plain twined bundle warp border. The warp stems are bent sharply over, usually in pairs, and are twined about the succeeding pairs. These stems, as the twining progresses, form two bundles between which are included in each case the succeeding pairs of upright stems. Each pair of these stems is at the same time bent down, joining that bundle of stems which passes to the rear or behind the other bundle, the outer surface of the basket being in view. This gives a simple plain twining of two bundles of warp sticks with no vertical projection of warp above the twined border as shown in pl. 30, fig. 1. It sometimes happens that a basket maker will not use both of each pair of warp stems, but will cut off one, thus reducing the size of each bundle used in twining. This has been noticed for instance in such large openwork granaries as the one shown in pl. 26, fig. 3.

While this same principle of manipulation is involved in the majority of the borders found upon openwork burden baskets and upon flat or hemispherical openwork baskets of the sifter type, many of these differ in having more than one row of twining warp stem bundles, and in having more than two stems in each group. Most have their warp stems gathered in groups of threes and bent into three rows of warp-twining as in pl. 26, figs. 1, 2; but baskets with as many as four rows of twining and four warp stems in each group have also been found. The essential features of all these methods are the same, but in some, for instance the border with three rows of twining and with warp stems grouped in threes, there is considerable variation in the exact manipulation of the stems. Each group of three warp stems is included between the two bundles of twining lowest down. Into this lowest row of twining bundles, however, one of the stems is often incorporated. A second may be taken up in the next row and the third in the top row. This is the most usual though not the universal method. The other methods found are as follows: All three warp stems may be carried up to the second or even to the top row. In the first case the second and third stems are carried up to the top row and usually the second is here incorporated, the third being cut off even with the top or rim of the basket, though both may be incorporated into the top row of twining bundles. On the other hand it may be that neither is incorporated but both cut off even with the rim. So far no case of a border in which two of the warp sticks are incorporated in the second row of twining bundles has been found. In case all the sticks are carried up to the top row, one only may be incorporated with that row, the other two being cut off, or two may be incorporated into the top row and one cut off. No case of all three being incorporated into the top row has as yet been found. In the instances where the warp stems are carried up to the second or to the top row, the lower rows are formed of bundles of weft stems inserted like the ordinary weft elements in the body of the basket.

Though the most usual method is the one first mentioned, in which one stem disappears into one of the twining bundles in each row, and ordinarily a basket has but the one border arrangement, there are certain cases in which nearly all of the several methods mentioned are found on the same basket. Further there are often placed close together just below the rows of bundles of warp sticks twined about each other, several rows of plain twining as is shown in pl. 30, fig. 1. This on an openwork basket, where the spaces are comparatively large, gives the region about the immediate border a very different appearance from that presented by the remainder of the basket, though in reality there is no different principle of weaving involved.

The second general type of border used on openwork baskets is what may be termed the braided and twined warp border as shown in pl. 30, fig. 2. As seen from the outer surface of the basket, this is a border in which two, three, or four warp sticks are together bent over sharply toward the right and passed in front of or outside the next group of the same number, then inside or behind the following group. As they pass behind this second group they join one of the two bundles of stems which are being twined about these groups of warp sticks, these bundles being simply the bent-over ends of former groups of warp sticks. Having joined the bundle they pass diagonally downward and reappear in front of the next group of warp sticks, this bundle being twined with the other so as to include the successive groups.

Thus by this plain twining of these bundles each disappears behind one group of warp sticks and reappears in front of the next group, giving the appearance of the twining of two large bundles of stems just below the rim of the basket, which itself has the appearance of being bordered with braided groups of warp sticks. In reality this is not a true braiding, though superficially it has the appearance of such a manipulation. This is chiefly used as the border of fish traps such as are shown in pl. 27, figs. 2, 4.

Upon the double fish trap shown in pl. 27, fig. 6, the same general method of manipulation at the border is shown. This border, however, differs from the one just described in that there are really two separate baskets which must be united by this border weave into one. To accomplish this the alternate warp sticks of each basket are cut off at the rim. This being done in both the large outer and the small inner basket, two of each set of our warp sticks are left in each case. The two on the outer larger basket and the corresponding two on the inner smaller one are united and form a set of four sticks which are then manipulated as has just been described.

In both the ordinary twined bundle warp border and the braided and twined warp border there are two methods of disposing of the ends of the warp sticks which remain after the last round of twining is finished. They are usually simply bound down to the edge of the rim of the basket with a willow stem or a piece of string, as is shown in pl. 25, figs. 5, 6, and pl. 26, fig. 3. They may, however, be braided together and the braid bound down in a similar manner, or the braid may be passed down below the lowest row of twining bundles and then passed two or three times in and out among the warp sticks in order to secure it. One notable exception to this careful securing of the ends of the remaining warp sticks to the rim of the basket is found in the double fish trap above referred to. Here these ends are simply bound securely together but are not fastened to the rim itself (pl. 27, fig. 6). At the same point on the basket also the inner and outer parts of it are not attached by having the warp sticks woven into a common border as was above described. On the contrary each has a separate border of bundles of warp

stems twined together, thus leaving a section of the border eight
or ten inches in length along which the two parts of the basket
are not attached.   As elsewhere explained in the present paper,
this fish basket is set as a trap in a brush wier built across a
stream, and the fish swim into it through the small opening in the
center of the inner conical basket.   Once within they rarely find
their way back through the same small opening.   It would also
be very difficult, if not quite impossible, for a fisherman to empty
the trap through this opening in the center.   Emptying the trap
is, therefore, provided for by the open section at its border.
When the trap is set, the edges of this open section together with
the projecting bundle of stems above referred to are bound together to prevent the fish from spreading them apart and es-
caping.   When it is desired to empty the trap this binding is cut
and the trap turned bottom upwards so that the fish fall out
through the opening at the border.

Another form of border finish used upon openwork baskets,
but very rarely met with, is that shown in pl. 30, fig. 3.   This
may be called a simple turned down warp border.   In this border
the warp stems are turned sharply over and pass on the outer
surface of the basket to the third warp stick on the right.   Here
the end of the stick which is being turned down is included between the strands of the topmost row of the plain twining of
which the whole basket consists.   The end of each one of these
warp sticks after being bound in this manner is cut off, only a
short projection being left on each below this last row of plain
twining.

### WICKERWORK.

Wickerwork, which has heretofore not been reported from
California, is found among the Pomo as the weave of a single
kind of basket, the handled seed-beater of the form shown in
pl. 24, fig. 1.   This is the only occurrence of this weave among
the Pomo, but it is almost always employed in making this particular form of basket.   Plain twining is however sometimes
used in seed-beaters, especially the form shown in pl. 24, fig. 4.
This twined seed-beater is made only in the northern part of the
territory occupied by the Northern division of the Pomo, and is

apparently due to the influence of contact with Athapascan and
Yuki peoples to the north.

## COILING.

The Pomo practice two methods of coiling, that upon a single-
rod foundation and that upon a three-rod foundation.  In point
of numbers neither of these methods can be said to predominate,
but the finest baskets and those most prized by the Indians are of
the three-rod foundation.  Feather decoration above mentioned
is seldom used in connection with single-rod coiling, but is much
used with the three-rod foundation.  Coiled basketry is chiefly
confined to certain forms: elliptical or so-called boat-shaped, such
as is shown in pl. 20 and pl. 19, figs. 4-6; forms approaching
more or less closely to globose, examples of which are shown in
pl. 18, figs. 3-6; one which may be termed hemispherical, found
in the so-called sun basket and in such baskets as the one shown
in pl. 19, fig. 3; and a flaring funnel or truncated cone form,
such as is shown in pl. 19, figs. 1, 2, and pl. 18, fig. 2.

A coiling on two-rod foundation was reported by certain informants, who stated that only one individual ever made baskets
of this sort.  Upon finding and questioning the basket maker
herself, however, it was found that the idea was original with her
and that she had made only two or three baskets of this type,
so that so far as the Pomo in general are concerned coiling upon
a two-rod foundation does not enter seriously into consideration.

Likewise coiling upon a rod and welt foundation is not a
typical Pomo process.  This method is practiced only by the
Pomo of the Northeastern division and is undoubtedly due to the
association of these people with the Yuki to the northwest, where
this form of coiling is the typical one.  Owing to the small number of survivors of this group opportunity has been afforded of
examining but a very few of these baskets.  Foundations of three
rods and one welt, and foundations of two rods and four welts
have been found.

In connection with coiled basketry the method of starting the
foundation should be noted.  In nearly all baskets where the
coiling proceeds in concentric circles, that is, in all coiled basketry except the elliptical or so-called boat-shaped form,  the

foundation is begun with a small bundle of sedge or other pliable
fibre. The rigidity of the willow stems used as the regular foundation material makes it impossible to bend them so sharply as
is necessary for the first few circles of the coiling. To start a
basket in this manner the maker simply takes several pieces, say
eight inches or so in length, of the flexible fibre, and ties them into
a simple knot in the middle. She then begins the coiling of a
bundle made by bringing the portions of the fibres lying outside
the knot together about it, at the same time wrapping the successive coils with the flexible sedge, bulrush, or other fibre, just
as is done in the coiling with willow stems. Having reached the
end of this small foundation bundle of flexible fibres, the ends of
the first willow stems are trimmed to proper points and inserted,
and with these the coiling then proceeds. The laying of the
foundation in this manner is the nearest approach to a multiple
rod or splint foundation in basketry used by the Pomo, except
those of the Northeastern division, who made a rod and welt
coil after the manner of the Yuki, as above mentioned. In addition to this method the Pomo also start coiled baskets by means
of small twining knots of one of the several forms used in starting
regular twined ware. Particularly they use the methods shown
in pl. 15, figs. 1, 5, except that each of the rigid rods shown here
is replaced by several small sedge or other fibers. They also make
a more elaborate knot the outward appearance of which is that of
a square composed of a set of four smaller squares. The projecting ends of the pliable fibers are usually manipulated as described
above and form a coil, or they may be treated as warp elements
and other fibers twined about them in plain or three-strand
twining, or in three-strand braiding. This makes a small disc
of twining to which the first round of the coil of willow rods is
sewed. In very recent years another method of starting these
circular bottoms has been used. A disk shell bead is taken and
wrapped with fibers, the perforation in its center serving to ad-
mit the fibers and produce the same effect as the sewing or wrapping of a coil of fibers or rods. Upon this wrapped bead as a
center the rods are coiled in the manner above described.

In starting the coil for a basket of the elliptical or so-called
boat-shaped form, on the other hand, no pliable material is

needed.   One or four rods of willow, according as to the basket is to have a single or three-rod foundation are cut off the exact length desired for the first coil of the basket, and are laid as the beginning of the foundation.   In the case of a single-rod foundation basket the sewing or wrapping of the first coil is done directly upon the single short stick which forms the keel, so to speak.   In the case of the three-rod foundation basket of the elliptical form, however, the four short rods selected are ordinarily first wrapped completely with sedge or other flexible fiber to form a compact bundle, and it is upon this bundle of four rods that the first coil of the basket is made, the sewing or wrapping of the coil being done in the same manner as in the case of the single-rod foundation.

The process of this sewing or wrapping of the coils has been described in detail by Professor Mason,[7] but it may here be noted that the basket maker always makes the opening which is to receive the sewing fiber by a thrust of the awl from the outer toward the inner surface of the basket.   The sharpened free end of the sewing fiber is then inserted and pulled through to the inside of the basket.   It is then pulled very tightly and binds firmly the rods of that particular row of coiling.   The insertion of a new sewing fiber is made by passing the end of it under the one or three rods of the coil and drawing the fiber inward toward the inside of the basket until the end is just hidden from view from the outside.   The sewing element already in use is then passed for the last time through the coils in the regular way.   This element includes all the rods of the coil which is just being added and also one rod of the coil next lower so that as it binds the new and the old coil together it holds the newly inserted element very securely between the two coils.   The old sewing element is then cut off just even with the inner surface of the basket, the newly inserted sewing element is taken up, and the coiling and sewing progress as before.   The insertions as a result of this process are in many cases scarcely discernible on the inner surface and never so on the outer surface of a basket.

So far as the finishing of Pomo coiled basketry is concerned, the last coil about the opening is made in the same manner as all

---

[7] Op. cit., pp. 250-253.

others and shows at this place no new manipulation and no special attempt at ornamentation. It is noteworthy, however, that the ends of the rods in this last coil are in most cases trimmed down in such a manner as to give a tapering effect to the end of the coil, thus avoiding an abrupt ending. The only exception to this is in the case of baskets made by two or three excellent workers, who are able to finish the last coil at the opening in such a manner that it is practically impossible to find where the coil ends. The exact method by which this is accomplished has not yet been determined.

### COILING.

| English | Northern | Central | Eastern |
|---|---|---|---|
| Coiling | cibū′ | cbū′, ctū | kibū′k |
| Single-rod foundation | tsai, ba′m-tca | tsai, ha′i-tatū | tsai, xa′i-kalī |
| Three-rod foundation | ba′m-sūbū | kala′l-sībo | xa′i-xōmka |
| | | ha′i-sībo | |

In connection with manipulation in Pomo basketry, it should be noted that as one looks at the outer surface of the bottom of a basket, twining always progresses in a clockwise direction, while coiling progresses in a counter clockwise direction. These are apparently the most logical methods of manipulation. Since the actual handling of the pliable fibers in either twining or coiling is done with the right hand, the left hand being employed in holding the rigid elements about which the flexible ones are being twined or coiled. In the case of twining, in which the progression is clockwise, the left hand is free to grasp the basket firmly and to hold in place the two or three warp sticks about which the weft elements have just passed, thus preventing the drawing of these out of alignment by the tension on the weft elements and at the same time not causing the left hand to interfere with the right as would be the case if the progression was counter clockwise or in a direction toward the left hand. Correspondingly, in coiling the fact that the progression is counter clockwise and that the unwrapped foundation sticks consequently project toward the left where the left hand can most easily grasp them firmly and hold them in position at the same time it is holding the basket securely seems to be a logical procedure. However, while these are the directions of progression found among the Pomo, it must be remembered that they are not the universal ones, but that considerable variation is shown among different peoples, as has been pointed out by Professor A. L. Kroeber in his "Ethnography of the Cahuilla Indians."[8]

## FORMS.

Pomo baskets show great variety of form. Among the larger baskets the conical form is found chiefly in burden baskets designed to be carried upon the back by means of a woven net, the weight being supported by a band passing over the forehead. These baskets are made in tightly woven plain twining and diagonal twining, as shown in pl. 22, as well as in openwork plain-twining, shown in pl. 26, figs. 1, 2. One specimen also of a three-strand twined burden basket has been found, but this is very exceptional. Coiled basketry is never made in this form.

The greater number of Pomo burden baskets do not approach so nearly the form of a perfect cone as do the burden baskets of certain other California peoples, for instance the Miwok of the southern Sierra region. There are, to be sure, Pomo burden baskets which are almost perfectly conical, but in most cases the bottom of the basket, that is the point of the cone, is very considerably rounded. Further, one side of the basket is also flattened, this being the side designed to rest on the back. By some informants it is said that this flattening is intentional and that the baskets are woven thus, but by other informants it is said that the flattening comes through use. Inasmuch, however, as in most new baskets this flattening appears, it seems probable that the former explanation is the correct one.

Forms approaching a truncated cone are quite common among the coiled baskets, but do not occur in twined ware. This form may vary from a true truncated cone to forms with very much incurved and others with very bulging sides. In all cases these truncated cones rest upon the smaller end as a base, the upper, larger end being entirely open. Examples of baskets of this general form are shown in pl. 18, fig. 2, and pl. 19, figs. 1, 2.

Hemispherical baskets of several kinds are also found. In this form both coiling and twining are used. Most notable among

---

[8] Present series, VIII, 49, 50, 1908.

the hemispherical coiled baskets is the three-rod so-called sun basket, which is entirely covered with red feathers and ornamented with bangles of clam and abalone shell. An example of an ordinary three-rod coiled basket of this form is shown in pl. 19, fig. 3. Large open-work baskets of the hemispherical form used for sifting and as general utensils are made in plain twining, lattice twining, and three-strand twining, as shown in pl. 25, figs. 1, 3, 6. Also a small basket used especially for the purpose of sifting acorn meal is made in forms varying between the hemispherical and the plate-form. This basket may be either provided on the bottom with a string loop (pl. 23, fig. 5) which passes around the hand and serves to hold it firmly, or with a small wooden peg (pl. 23, fig. 6), which is grasped between the second and third fingers for the same purpose. This small sifter is most frequently made in plain twining. With this hemispherical form should also probably be classed the mortar or grinding basket, examples of which are shown in pl. 23, figs. 3, 4, though it varies from a true hemisphere to a truncated cone. This basket, used with a pestle for grinding all kinds of vegetable foods, has a large upper opening, bound and strengthened by a heavy wooden hoop, and a smaller opening at the bottom, which rests upon a flat stone.

The most commonly occurring utensil is the basket which may be termed plate-form, shown in pl. 23, figs. 1, 2 and variously known as pan, plaque, etc. It is made in plain, diagonal, and lattice twining, and serves all the useful purposes of a pan among the whites. Baskets of this form range in size from very small to very large, the latter being used chiefly for parching seeds by means of hot coals. Upon rare occasions a coiled basket, usually of single-rod foundation, is made in this plate form, but such are said by the Indians not to have been extensively used in aboriginal times. They are probably patterned after the basketry of the Wintun immediately to the east.

The more or less cylindrical basket, examples of which are shown in pl. 17, figs. 3, 6, and used chiefly for the purpose of cooking acorn mush and other foods, is also very commonly found among the Pomo. Baskets used for this purpose are invariably of the three more commonly occurring twined weaves. Coiled baskets such as that shown in pl. 18, fig. 6, which approach the cylindrical form, are like all other coiled baskets, never used by the Pomo for purposes of cooking. The Maidu, Wintun, Yuki and other California peoples to the south, except the Pomo, use coiled baskets almost exclusively for cooking purposes. The greater number of the large openwork baskets, such as the one shown in pl. 26, fig. 3, and used for the purpose of storing acorns or other foods are also of the cylindrical form, though they sometimes approach the spherical. Smaller openwork baskets, such as the one shown in pl. 25, fig. 2, are used for storing small objects like basket materials, bone awls, etc.

Passing through all gradations of this cylindrical type with its rounded bottom, a spherical form is reached, such as is shown in pl. 16, fig. 3, pl. 17, fig. 4 and pl. 18, fig. 5, in which the only deviation from an almost perfect sphere is the comparatively slight flattening of the bottom necessary to make a surface upon which the basket may rest, and the comparatively small opening at the top. Baskets of this kind are frequently found in plain and diagonal twined weaving, and also in both forms of coiling. The coiled and many of the twined baskets of this type are used for ceremonial or other purposes not strictly governed by utility. The same is true of the spheroidal form (pl. 16, fig. 2, and pl. 18, fig. 1), which with very much flattened top and bottom grades almost imperceptibly into the spherical. The spheroidal form is made in the same weaves as the spherical.

A special form of basket is that resembling the spheroidal, but with a decided narrowing just above the flat base, so that it presents the effect of a spheroid slightly raised from the supporting surface. But very few of these baskets have been seen and these were all in three-rod coiling. The Indians say that this form is not an aboriginal one, but has been made at the request of the whites. The same is true of one or two baskets seen which had a pedestal or foot resembling that of a goblet or cake stand.

Elliptical or so-called boat-shaped baskets, such as those shown in pl. 20, and pl. 19, figs. 4-6, occur in the two methods of coiling and in almost every variation of form, from globes with slightly compressed sides to very narrow and long baskets. In some the opening, always elliptical, is almost as large as the body of the basket itself, but in most it is much smaller. This particular form of basket, although made quite commonly among the Pomo, is very rarely found elsewhere. They seem to have been used as gifts or, particularly in the case of those of very large size, as ceremonial baskets and as storage baskets for ceremonial and all other important objects, except foods.

Fish-traps, all of which are made by the men in coarse plain-twined weaving, present certain specialized forms. One, illustrated in pl. 27, fig. 3, somewhat resembles a half cylinder. This trap is used in shallow streams for catching small fish. Another, shown in fig. 5 of the same plate is used only in the vicinity of Clear lake, and has the form of a truncated cone with openings at both ends. This trap is used in shallow muddy water. The fisherman grasps the upper or smaller end, and as he wades along plants the trap here and there in the hope of catching the fish unawares. As he feels the fish striking against the side of the trap in its endeavor to swim away, he reaches through the upper small opening and removes the fish with his hand. A third form, shown in fig. 6 of this plate, more or less approaches the conical, but has a small funnel set in the opening. This trap is placed in a wier, so that as the fish swim along in their endeavor to get up or down stream they come upon the funnel and pass in through the small inner opening into the rear of the trap and are unable to find their way out. The fourth form of fish trap, that shown in fig. 2 of this plate, is a long, usually cylindrical, one with flaring mouth, but without a retaining funnel as in the cast just mentioned. This trap is also set in a wier in the same manner. In addition to the long cylindrical type mentioned above, some of these traps, such as the one shown in fig. 4, are made in the form of a very long slender cone. Still another trap, resembling in form the long cylindrical fish trap, is the one used for catching quail. It is in from two to five or six sections of six feet or so each. The one here shown (pl. 28, fig. 3) has four sections with a total length of twenty-four feet. The diameter of this trap varies from four to six or seven inches. It is set in a long brush fence, toward which the quail are driven, especially in wet weather. The diameter of the trap is so small that the quail cannot conveniently turn around when once they

have entered. Another trap constructed upon the same principal as that for taking quail is the small woodpecker trap (pl.
27, fig. 1). By binding this trap after dark over the entrance
to a woodpecker's nest all the birds are entrapped as they endeavor to come out on the following morning.

Still another basket of hemispherical form, which like the
above mentioned hemispherical fish trap is made by the men, is
the cradle or baby basket (pl. 24, fig. 2). The child is seated in
this cradle and after being thoroughly wrapped is securely bound
with the lashings shown in the figure. At the present time the
child is wrapped in ordinary cloth but aboriginally finely shred-
ded tule was used for the purpose. The hoop which projects
out toward the front serves the double purpose of a handle by
which to lift the basket and of a support for a screen to keep
off insects and the bright light. From this hoop also dangle
various objects which serve to amuse the child, whose arms are
tightly bound and who might otherwise become more restless.
The broad woven band at the rear of the basket passes over the
forehead or chest of the mother and supports the basket upon
her back in the same manner as the head band of a burden basket.

One other form of basket found among the Pomo is the seed-
beater with a handle (pl. 24, fig. 1). This is usually made in
wickerwork, the only basket made in this weave by the Pomo.
Wickerwork is of rare occurrence on the Pacific slope and has
not heretofore been reported from California. While this is the
typical form of Pomo seed-beater there is another made by the
Pomo living in the extreme northern part of the territory of the
Northern division. As shown in pl. 24, fig. 4, this is quite conical,
made in plain twining upon radial warp sticks, and with a handle
consisting of a number of sticks inserted in the interstices at
intervals from the conical point to the edge along one side of the
basket. To these are added the few warp sticks covered by and
immediately adjacent to them and the whole bundle is bound with
grape vine or other binding material. A notable feature of the
handle is the manner of this binding, which consists in all cases
of an ordinary wrapping near the base of the handle and then a
sort of spiral tying, along the rest of its length. The binding

material passes diagonally from one to the next of the outer
sticks of the handle, in each case inclosing a single stick in a
simple wrap of the binding material. Sometimes it does not inclose in this manner each one of the outer sticks but only alternate
ones. All of the warp sticks except the few covered by and immediately adjacent to the handle are broken off at a distance of
half an inch or so from the uppermost row of twining. This
gives the basket the appearance of being bordered with a row
of projecting points. Such projection of the warp sticks is
typical of Pomo twined basketry but in this case it is of unusual
length.

## FORMS.

| *English* | *Northern* | *Central* | *Eastern* |
|---|---|---|---|
| Basket (generic) | pīka' | ŏ'nma | ca'di, cat |
| Conical burden | | | |
|   Closely woven, pl. 22. | bidji' | ptcī | bŭgŭ' |
|   Openwork of peeled rods, pl. 26; 1 | bito'i-tsoi, tsoi | īka'l | tso'i |
|   Openwork of unpeeled rods, pl. 26; 2 | ha'i-dŭkal | tcama'ū | tsoi |
| Truncated cone, pl. 18; 2, pl. 19; 1, 2 | ŭyĭ'l-tŏ | ctŭ'-ptci | tīrī'-bŭgŭ |
| Hemispherical, pl. 19; 3 | batĭ'bŏom | ctŭ | |
| Openwork, sifter type, pl. 25; 3 | caka'n-tīn | sa'l-stin | cala'p |
|   Culinary, pl. 25; 4-6 | caka'n | sal | |
| Plate-form, pl. 23; 1 | dala' | nasŭ' | dala' |
| Plate-form, small, pl. 23; 2 | dala'kan | tŏ'ŭ | te'ŭ |
| Plate-form, sifter, pl. 23; 5-6 | | sŭ'kan | |
| Cylindrical, pl. 17; 3 | too'-pīka | ta'kan | |
| Cylindrical, small | dem | cee't | |
| Spherical, pl. 17; 4 | pīka'-tcadŏl | cee't-tcibūtcibū | gŭmŭ'Lŭ |
| Elliptical or boat-shaped, pls. 20, and 19; 4-6 | cīlŏ' | kala'cūna | xala'cūna |
| Cylindrical fish trap, pl. 27; 2, 4 | ka'kŏi | ba'iya-hakŏ | xa'xŏi |
| Conical fish trap, pl. 27; 6 | bŭka'l | ha'kŏ | bŭxa'l |
| Truncated cone fish trap, pl. 27; 5 | | ca'-mtce | ca'-mĭdje |
| Half-cylinder fish trap, pl. 27; 3 | | tsada't | tsada'r |
| Quail trap, pl. 28, fig. 3 | caka'ga-hakŏi | caka'ga-hakŏi | cag'a'x-hakŏi |
| Handled seed-beater, pl. 24; 1 | batŭ' | batŭ' | batŏ' |
| Open-work storage, pl. 26; 3 | pase' | itī't | dĭtī'r |

| English | Northern | Central | Eastern |
|---|---|---|---|
| Openwork storage, small | | tso'i | bitsŭ'l |
| Mortar, pl. 29; 3, 4 | mĭdje' | mtce | mĭdje' |
| Cradle, pl. 24; 2 | sĭka' | | xa'i-katŏli |
| Feathered basket (any form) | ta'-pĭka, i'pĭka | ta'-stŏl | ta'-sĭtŏl yĭi'-cat |

## ORNAMENTATION.

The ornamentation of Pomo basketry may be placed under two general heads, the first comprising all designs and patterns worked into the basket proper by the use of different kinds and colors of fibrous materials, the second comprising what may be termed auxiliary ornamentation or the various forms of decoration produced by means of feathers, beads, and bits of abalone shell. The subject of auxiliary ornamentation has already been spoken of under the head of basket materials, where, in connection with the sources of the various feather and shell materials, their use upon baskets of certain forms and devoted to certain uses, and the general method of their manipulation have been treated. In passing, however, it should also be mentioned that in a great measure, except where the surface of the basket is entirely covered with feathers, no attempt is made to work out a pattern in the feathers themselves, their use being chiefly secondary to the pattern worked out in the fibre. Often the red feathers of the redheaded woodpecker are scattered at frequent intervals over the white part, or what may be considered the groundwork of the basket; they thus outline and bring more prominently to notice the pattern which is worked out in black, or sometimes red, fibre material. At other times these or other feathers are scattered in this manner over the entire surface of the basket regardless of the pattern. However, where the surface is thickly covered with feathers the designs which are worked out in the feathers are of course the same as the designs in the fiber materials of the baskets, although on account of the nature of the feathers it seems impossible to make other than simple patterns. At any rate the more difficult pattern are never found.

Pomo baskets, as before mentioned, are made of fiber materials in three colors, white, black, and red. It is almost invariably the case that the white material is used as a background or surface upon which to work out a pattern in black or red. A few cases, however, have been found where the portion of the pattern made in the white material, instead of that in the colored material, was named by the informant. In all such cases the white was as much or more conspicuous than the colored, as for instance in a case of diagonal zigzags in which the white and black or red zigzag lines alternated. No instances have as yet been found among the Pomo of baskets with backgrounds of a colored fiber and with a comparatively small pattern in white, as is quite often the case among the Yuki immediately north of the Pomo.

DESIGN ARRANGEMENT.

One of the noteworthy features of Pomo basketry is the fact that designs are arranged in several ways, instead of in only one or two as is the case with most California peoples. The two principal methods of arrangement are the horizontal one, in which the design is arranged in a band or circle about the basket, and the diagonal one, which on account of the curved surface of the basket gives the appearance of a spiral. Instances of these are shown in pl. 16, figs. 4 and 2 respectively. Less frequently occurring arrangements are what may be termed the vertical, in which designs are placed vertically, and the individual, without any apparent reference to other figures upon the basket. Examples of these arrangements are shown respectively in pl. 18, fig. 5, and in the first four figures of pl. 29. Still another method of arrangement, the crossing, which should really be considered as an amplification of the diagonal, is shown in pl. 17, fig. 6, and in pl. 28, fig. 1. Closely related to this is the arrangement shown in pl. 16, fig. 6, and pl. 22, fig. 4, where the pattern, in both these cases of large triangular figures, is so arranged that the corners of each touch corners of those nearest in such a manner that the rows of figures appear either as diagonal and parallel or as crossing. This arrangement might also be considered as superimposed horizontal rows of figures. Very elaborate and effective patterns are produced in this manner.

In connection with this matter of design arrangement it is notable that certain of them are not only much more frequent than others, but also that the proportions in which these different arrangements appear vary considerably, according to the technique. The following table, based upon one hundred and twenty-three twined and one hundred and forty-three coiled baskets, shows the approximate per cents of the various methods of design arangement in twining and coiling respectively.

|  | Horiz. | Diag. | Crossing | Vertical | Individ. |
|---|---|---|---|---|---|
| Twined | 70 | 25 | 5 | 0 | 0 |
| Coiled | 40 | 30 | 10 | 15 | 5 |

The horizontal or banded arrangement prevails in both twined and coiled basketry, being that found on a large per cent of the former and on the latter in a smaller though very considerable per cent. This arrangement is particularly noticeable on burden, and cylindrical or spherical cooking baskets, both of which are made only in the twined weaves. Practically equal per cents of diagonal patterns are found in twining and coiling, and small per cents only of crossing patterns are found in both. No vertical or individual arrangements appear in twined basketry, and they are rarely met with in coiling. Thus it appears that Pomo basketry is characterized in the matter of its design arrangement particularly by the horizontal and diagonal methods.

As regards the single and three-rod foundations of coiled basketry no particular arrangement of the patterns predominates, but in twining certain arrangements are more frequent on baskets of a particular weave than upon others. Upon plain and upon lattice twined baskets the arrangement is almost wholly horizontal. Upon diagonal-twined it is largely diagonal, with a small per cent. of crossing. A few have patterns covering the entire surface of the basket. The horizontal arrangement only is found upon baskets of the three-strand twined weaves.

In connection with their designs, particularly the horizontal ones, the Pomo seem to have had the rather unusual custom of purposely leaving a break or opening in the pattern, and it is almost, if not quite, impossible to find a basket with its patterns arranged in horizontal bands in which they all run continuously around the entire basket. There is almost always in one of the bands, and usually in all of them, a larger or smaller opening somewhere about it. In some cases these openings are very small indeed, being marked by but a slight difference in a few stitches, while at other times they are broad and filled with an elaborate pattern of a kind entirely different from the general one to either side. Instances of such openings are shown in pl. 17, fig. 3, and pl. 23, figs. 1, 3, 5. This break is called by the Northern Pomo daū and hamaka'm, by the Central Pomo ha'mda and ham, and by the Eastern Pomo hwa. That this opening is not left by accident is shown from the fact that many baskets have bands of designs which, had they been completed entirely of the same figures, would have made perfect patterns. Further, the Indians themselves maintain that these breaks are left in the design on account of their belief that the maker of a basket without such a break will become blind. They also say that the first people were instructed by Coyote, the culture hero, to leave such breaks and that the instruction has rarely been forgotten or disregarded. They even give legendary accounts of women who have in times past neglected to leave such openings in their patterns and who have actually paid the penalty of blindness. Such accounts and explanations from the Indians must of course be taken as effect rather than cause in considering the probable origin of this custom. There is reason to believe that the true origin of the dau is in technique and that the explanations now given by the Indians accounting for its existence are entirely secondary. Having once originated, however, such explanations would tend to more firmly fix the custom, and to cause the dau to appear where it might otherwise be omitted.

Upon some baskets whose patterns are arranged spirally there appear small odd designs between the spirals or within one of the large elements of one of them. Some informants give the same names to these as to the breaks in the banded patterns. Others, however, recognize no connection between the two. A basket upon which both of these occur is shown in pl. 16, fig. 5.

Short pieces of the quill of the yellowhammer or red-shafted flicker are found in many baskets at one or more points over the surface. The insertion of these is also connected with the idea of blindness and general ill-luck. They are placed in the basket by a woman upon the approach of a menstrual period if for any reason she does not wish to cease work upon the basket. Traditional belief requires that a basket maker cease all such work as well as observe many other restrictions in the matter of eating, handling certain objects, etc., at such a time. If, however, she wishes to continue the work upon a basket this may be done, provided first a few stitches of the quill of the yellowhammer be inserted in the basket at the point where she is at work. In the majority of cases, however, a menstruating woman ceases all such work, which accounts for the fact that not all baskets show the small pieces of quill, and that very few baskets show more than one or two of them.

## ELEMENTAL DESIGNS.

In considering the subject of Pomo designs and design names a very sharp distinction must be made between a design element or simple elemental figure, and a pattern or complex figure composed sometimes of a single design element repeated, and sometimes of two or more of these simple elemental figures combined to form a complex whole. An example of the former may be seen in fig. 1 or fig. 127, while examples of the latter may be seen in figs. 55, 34, 36, etc. In naming designs and patterns the Pomo themselves make just such distinctions, with the result that their names may be conveniently arranged under the two heads: names of design elements, and names of patterns. The former are simple names of well known natural or artificial objects, geometric figures, and the like; while for a combination of these simple elemental figures to form a complex pattern they give a name which is more of a descriptive sentence or phrase-name than a simple word, since it gives the principal, at least, of the constituent elements and mentions the relation in which they stand one to another. Of course there is a certain variability in the names given to the same design element by different informants, and still more is this true of the names given to the complex patterns. To a large extent, however, what appears a considerable variation in names is found upon investigation to correspond to the differences of dialect, so that within any one dialectic group the naming of elements and patterns is fairly uniform with all informants, though, as would be expected, there are variations among individuals of the same group.

### Triangular Elements.

The most frequently occurring design element is the *arrow-head,* called by the Northern Pomo katca'k, by the Central Pomo katca', and by the Eastern Pomo kaga' or xaga'. The arrowhead design is at all times a triangle, though the exact form of the triangle varies greatly. While triangles of other forms are sometimes used the isosceles triangle predominates. The majority of these have the angle at the apex 90 degrees. Figures 1 to 63 show the various forms of triangles and also a few of the many combinations of triangles with triangles and of triangles with other figures. To almost all of these triangular figures the name arrowhead is given, though a few, which will be noted below, are more often called by other names. Several of these other designations, such as sharp points, etc., apparently carry to the Indian mind the same general idea as arrowhead.

The design shown in fig. 1, a band of isosceles right triangles, placed at comparatively great distances from each other, was called by some Northern Pomo informants dīta'ska, *spotted,* though by another informant it was named dita's tcidī'yemūl, *spot tcidī'yemūl,* and by still another datī'pka, *sharp points.* Central Pomo informants gave in most cases katca'-dalaū, *arrowhead-half.* Katca'-mtil tciltaū, *arrowhead-slender stuck-on,* was also given. Eastern informants gave kaga', *arrowhead,* and kaca'icai kūdja, *butterfly small.* Triangles arranged with such wide spacing are of rare occurrence, but two cases being thus far noted.

A single case of pairs of isosceles right triangles arranged in a band about a basket, in the manner shown in fig. 2, was found. The Northern and Eastern informants gave the unqualified name *arrowhead* to this design; but Central informants differed, one calling it *arrowhead,* another *arrowhead-half,* katca'-dalaū, and a third *arrowhead-half stuck-on,* katca-dalaū tcī'ltaū.

Bands of design made up of isosceles right triangles arranged with short intervals between their bases and with their apexes pointing downward, as is shown in fig. 3, occasionally occur. In all three of the Pomo divisions these are called *arrowhead*. In the Northern they  were also called by one informant *butterfly*, kaca'icai, and by another *turtle-back*, kawï'na-tcïdik. By other informants they were called *pine-tree design*, kawa'ca datoï. By Central Pomo informants they were also called *arrowhead-half*, katca'-dalaū, and *turtle-neck*, kawï'na-ūtca. By those of the Eastern dialect they were also called *arrowhead-half*, kaga'-daLaū, as well as *butterfly*, kaca'icai. This design is of but rare occurrence.

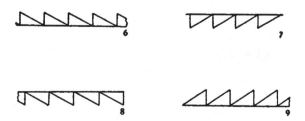

Bands of isosceles right triangles arranged with their bases touching each other and either with their apexes pointing up or pointing down, as in figs. 4 and 5, are sometimes found. These are called by the Northern Pomo, in addition to the common term *arrowhead*, which is however not often applied to these particular figures, *butterfly*, kaca'icai, and *large spots*, dapo'kka. One Central informant gave these designs the name *turtle-neck*, kawïn'a-ūtca, at the same time, however, stating that the design was unfinished. Eastern informants called this design *butterfly*, kaca'icai.

In figs. 6, 7, 8 and 9 four different arrangements of an ordinary right triangle are shown. By Northern Pomo informants these figures were called *design pointed*, datoï ditï'pka. By informants speaking the Central dialect they were called *arrow-head-sharp*, katca'-mset, though by another informant figs. 6, 7, and 8 were called *zigzag-half*, tsīyo'tsīyo-balaū, fig. 9 being called by her *arrowhead-half band*, katca'-dalaū ctot. By Eastern informants these figures were called kaga'-dīset, kaga signifying *arrowhead* and dīse't meaning any objects, *whether pointed or otherwise, which project or stick up*. They were also called *arrowhead-half*, kaga'-daLaū, and *arrowhead sharp*, kaga'-mīset. Designs made of these figures are very rarely met with.

One instance, fig. 10, was noted of right triangles similar to those above mentioned but arranged in a double instead of a single row. Two Northern Pomo informants gave the name datoī dītī'pka tcacītemūl, *design pointed, going-around and meeting (plural)*. According to a Central informant it is called katca'-dalaū ctot, *arrowhead-half band*. Eastern informants differ between xaga' kama, *arrowhead mark*, and kaca'icai, *butterfly*.

One case of these right triangles at considerable distances from one another was also found, but in this case the triangles are combined with another element so that their bases rest upon a line. This design is shown in fig. 11. Northern informants call it katca'k datsai-banem, *arrowhead broadband* (literally broad placed or put on). One Central informant gave the name *arrowhead-sharp*, katca'-mset, to this design, while another called it *eye-half (plural)*, ū'ī-balaū-ai. No name was obtained for it in the Eastern dialect.

Occurring very rarely are such designs as those shown in figs. 12 and 13, in which the apex of each isosceles triangle touches the middle of the base of the triangle next to the right or to the left according as the design points toward the one direction or the other. Designs such as these, whether arranged horizontally, as here, or vertically, as in figs. 14, 15 and 16, usually bear the name *turtle-back* or *turtle-neck*. All these five designs are called by the Northern Pomo kawī'na-tcīdik or kawī'na-kū, *turtle-back* or *turtle-neck*, the former being more often used. Among the Central and Eastern Pomo they are called *turtle-neck*, kawī'na-ūtca and kana'dīhwa-koī respectively. There are however informants who give these figures different names. Fig. 12 was called by two Northern informants bice-yee nat datoī, *deer-breast nat design*. Fig. 13 was called by the same informants datoī datīpka

tcacdīmūl, *design sharp-points, going around and meeting (singular)*. Figs. 14 and 15 were called by them also kawa'ca datoī, *pine-tree design*, while they gave as other names for fig. 15 bice-yee nat, *deer-breast nat*, and datīpka ū'yūl dana daienka, *sharp-points upward rub (?) placed close together in a row*. Correspondingly for fig. 16 they gave yo'wil dana datīpka, *downward rub (?) sharp-points*. One Eastern informant called the design of fig. 14 xaga'-miLau, *arrowhead split-open*. For the design of fig. 15 the same informant gave on one occasion *butterfly*, kaca'icai, while another mentioned xaitsa'k kama. Xaitsa'k may be approximately translated as *stretcher*, since in its use it most nearly resembled a stretcher for carrying the wounded. It was made of green limbs woven together and was used for transporting an invalid or anyone who might have been injured, for instance, while hunting.

Figure 16 shows one of the very few hollow figures used on Pomo basketry. Practically all the remaining figures are what

may be called solid or filled figures. The design shown in this particular figure has been found so far on but a very few baskets. While it is ordinarily given the same name as the similar figures just mentioned, it is worthy of note that it also has other names. For instance the Central Pomo call it pcē'-meō kawī'na-ūtca, *deer-back turtle-neck*. Among the Eastern Pomo it was called by one informant

*tū'ntūn* wīnalīhempke, *ants crossing*, by another bū'-dilē wīnalīhempke, *potato-forehead crossing.* By potato is meant what is
called "Indian potatoes," the bulbs, tubers and corms of the
many species of bulbous and tubrous rooted plants which grow
in the Pomo country. Exactly what is meant by potato-forehead
is not certain, for the Indians themselves differ in their explanations of the term. Some say it refers to a protuberance on the
upper surface of a corm and of some bulbs also, while others
maintain that it refers to a protuberance on the bottom instead
of on the top. In the schematic design shown in figure 16 the
reason for these various names is not apparent.

The nature of the surface upon which this design must be
worked, the basket being built up as it is of consecutive coils,
renders it impossible to make a perfectly straight slanting line.
The best means therefore of making a slanting line is to make a
succession of small squares or rectangles, each coming in a little
nearer toward the apex of the triangle than the one below. If
these squares or rectangles are of fair size they are called by the
Central Pomo deer-back, and by the Eastern Pomo potato-forehead. If they are very small they are called ants by both, thus
accounting for the variation in the name of the design shown in
this particular figure. In the case of the Central dialect name
mentioned above, it is interesting to note that two names have
been combined. Deer-back turtle-neck names the small figures of
which the larger figure is composed and also the large figure as
a whole. The term wīna'līhempke, *crossing,* used by the Eastern
Pomo refers of course to the convergence of these lines of small
squares or rectangles. The designs of figs. 12 and 13 have so far
been found in but one instance each. That of fig. 14 has been
found twice, that of fig. 15 eight times, and that of fig. 16 four
times.

Isosceles right triangles arranged diagonally, as shown in

17

figs. 17, 18, 19, and 20, are found frequently. Only the design shown in fig. 20
is found alone as a distinct pattern. The
designs in all four of these figures are,
however, very frequently met with in com-
binations of elaborate patterns. In fact the most elaborate pat-

terns of all those found in Pomo basketry have these as their chief elements. Looking from the bottom toward the rim of a basket nearly all spiral designs progress toward the left. Therefore the most complex spiral patterns having any of the designs represented in these four figures as their chief elements have those shown in figs. 18 and 20 upon the upper and lower side of the

18

spiral respectively. Arranged between these two principal elements, which are in almost all cases of comparatively large size, may be almost any other element or combination of elements. Such a complex pattern is shown in fig. 55, where a zigzag element is placed between the two triangle elements. Only one case has so far been found of an ordinary spiral pattern having the elements represented in figs. 17 and 19 as components, this being the

19

only case of an ordinary spiral progressing upward toward the right instead of toward the left. The designs shown in these two figures do, however, have considerable use in such complex crossing patterns as those

in pl. 19, fig. 3, and pl. 17, fig. 6. Patterns of this kind are composed of two spiral designs, one progressing upward toward the left in the ordinary manner, the other progressing upward toward the right, thus causing them to cross each other. All four of the designs shown in these figures find still another use, namely, in what may be termed edging or bordering the large triangles of one of these spiral patterns. Such a bordering, employing the designs shown in figs. 17 and 19, is found in the complex pattern of fig. 55. In addition to these uses, one of the pairs of the four is sometimes employed as the center of a complex spiral pattern. Such a center is shown in fig. 56, in which the designs of figs. 18 and 20 are found. In a separate pattern, such as is shown in fig. 56, these elements are but rarely found. It is occasionally used however as the one filling the central spaces between the large diagonal rows of triangles, as is done by the zigzag in fig. 55. All these designs whether they are used as the primary elements in a complex pattern, or as the secondary elements in such a pattern, are called *arrow-*

*head* by the Pomo of all three divisions under consideration, though of course there are certain differences in naming them.

Used singly as the entire pattern of a basket the design shown in fig. 20 is usually called by the Central and Eastern Pomo  *arrowhead-half,* katca'-dalaū and kaga'-daLaū respectively. By Northern informants it was called datō'ī kata daienga, *design empty placed-close-together-in-a-row.* When used as the principal elements of a complex pattern the designs shown in figs. 17 and 20 are called by Central dialect informants *inward-arrowhead,* tca'l-katca, while those represented in figs. 18 and 19 are called by the same informants *outward-arrowhead,* ko'l-katca. The explanation obtained from them for these names was that in weaving such a design as that in fig. 17 or 20, where the apexes of the triangles point upward, each triangle is made successively shorter and shorter rows of fiber. Thus the work constantly progresses inward to the apex of the triangle. In the other designs, shown in figs. 18 and 19, where the apexes of the triangles point downward, the operation is reversed and each triangle is made up of a succession of rows ever increasing in length, thus progressing constantly outward from the apex to the base of the triangle. Such a distinction was not made by informants of the other two Pomo divisions, these designs being usually called by those of the Eastern dialect *arrowhead-half,* kaga'-daLaū, or in some cases *butterfly,* xaca'icai. By the questioned informants of the Northern dialect they were called in most cases datō'ī kata, *design empty,* or simply *arrowhead,* katca'k. The same names were also given to these designs when they appeared as secondary or auxiliary (figs. 55, 56) to the larger spirals or triangles.

As above stated, right triangles arranged as is shown in fig. 20 are occasionally used as the pattern of an entire basket, but  only one case of a double row of these triangles, such as is shown in fig. 21, has been been found. This design was called by two Northern Pomo informants datō'ī kata ūyūl daienga, *design empty upward placed-close-together-in-a-row.* By Central informants it was called *arrowhead,* katca', and also *arrowhead slender,* katca'-mtil. By Eastern informants it was called *butterfly,* xaca'icai.

22            23            24

Similar to the above mentioned arrangements of isosceles right triangles are found such patterns as those in figs. 22, 23, and 24. When the design shown in fig. 20 is used as the entire design of a basket it differs from these in that each diagonal row of isosceles right triangles is distinct and separate from the remaining rows, whereas in these cases each triangle touches at its three corners its neighbors. Thus they may be either considered as arranged horizontally or as arranged diagonally. These patterns are found arranged in bands or circles about the surface of a basket and vary from two to as many as four triangles in width. As shown in these figures the apexes may point either up or down, and they may be accompanied by a heavy bordering line, as is shown in fig. 24. These patterns are called by the Northern and Eastern Pomo *butterfly,* kaca'icai and xaca'icai respectively, while Central informants always called them *arrowhead-half,* katca'-dalaū. By one or two Northern informants these patterns were also called datŏ'ĭ kata, *design empty.* What is in reality the same as these patterns except that the triangular figures cover the entire surface of the basket instead of being arranged in bands is shown in pl. 16, fig. 6. This pattern occurs occasionally and, if unaccompanied by other elements, is called by the same names as the banded triangular patterns above mentioned.

One of the most frequently occurring arrangements of these isosceles right triangles is that shown in fig. 25. It rarely happens that a simple pattern exactly like that of this figure is found, but the great majority of banded or circular patterns are formed upon this as a base. All sorts of other design elements are combined to make the complete elaborate pattern. A noteworthy feature of

25

all patterns founded upon this as a base is that the apex of each triangle is so placed that if moved upward it would just fit the space between the two triangles above. No case has yet been noted in which the apexes of the opposing triangles were placed opposite each other. These large triangles, which form what may be termed the primary elements of the pattern, may be arranged as in fig. 25 with more or less space between their bases, or they may be so arranged that the points of their bases touch the adjacent triangles. The former is the more usual arrangement, however. As in the case of the main elements of the diagonal patterns of triangles, Central Pomo informants seemed to differentiate more sharply between these elements than did those of the Northern or Eastern Pomo divisions. By Northern informants both the upper and the lower triangles were usually called datŏ'ĭ kata, *design empty,* and by the Eastern Pomo *butterfly,* xaca'icai, or *arrowhead,* xaga'. Central informants, however, named separately the two sets of triangles, those in the lower row being called yŏ'-katca, *lower-arrowhead,* and those in the upper row ŭ'yŭ-katca, *above or upper-arrowhead.*

There are many combinations of these design elements with others. Three examples are shown in figs. 26, 27 and 28. The first is called by Northern informants datŏ'ĭ kata dilē katcak daienga, *design empty in-the-middle arrowheads placed-close-to-gether-in-a-row,* the second datŏ'ĭ kata xŏl-tŭ, datĭpka, *design empty on-both-sides sharp-points.* By Central informants such an exact distinction is not made, the first being called by them katca'-dalaŭ lēLan, *arrowhead-half in-the-center,* katca'-mset ctot, *arrowhead-sharp band,* or katca'-mtĭl ctot, *arrowhead slender band,* while the second was called katca'-dalaŭ ctot, *arrowhead-half band,* or kaca'icai ctot, *butterfly-band.* By Eastern informants the first was called xaca'icai dilē gaiya xaga dzīyŏ'dzīyŏ, *butterfly in-the-middle gaiya arrowhead zigzag* or simply xaga'-mĭset, *arrowhead-sharp,* or dzīyŏ'dzīyŏ dĭset, *zigzag projecting.*

The pattern of fig. 27 was called xaca′icai winalīhempke kalūtū-duk kōldaiyaūhmak, *butterfly crossing striped-watersnake meet-together* or simply xaga′-daLaū, *arrowhead-half*, or xaca′icai-diset, *butterfly-projecting*. The design of

fig. 28 is the same as that of fig. 27, except that the central design element consists of a double instead of a single row of small triangles which point up instead of down.

28

A pattern composed of large triangles combined with smaller ones but quite different in form from those

just discussed is shown in fig. 29. Here the smaller triangles used to border the larger ones are made an integral part of them so that each large triangle appears to

29

them so that each large triangle appears to have one smooth and one serrated side.

Other examples of such combinations are shown in figs. 30 and 31. In the former the band of large triangular figures is combined with the conventionalized design named after the club-shaped plume from the crest of the California quail. By the

30          31

Northern Pomo this pattern is called datŏ′ĭ kata xŏltū cakaga-kēya daien, *design empty on-both-sides quail-plumes collected.* A similar descriptive, though shorter, name was given by Eastern informants, who called this pattern xaca′icai hna caga′-xe, *butterfly and (or with) quail-plumes.* By all informants of the Central dialect this pattern was simply called *quail-plume band*, caka′ga-kēya ctot. In fig. 31 a rather unusual combination of triangles is shown. In fact this has thus far been found on but one basket. Information concerning it is lacking from the Northern and Eastern Pomo, but it was called by Central informants katca′-dalaū ctot lala tsīyŏ′tsīyŏ tcūwan, *arrowhead-half band in-the-middle zigzag stripe.* In this name curiously enough no mention is made of the smaller inner triangles themselves, only the white zigzag between these small triangles being noted.

Similar to these designs, yet different in that they lack the upper row of triangles placed with their apexes downward, are the patterns represented in figs. 32, 33, 34 and 35. Concerning the first no information was obtained from Northern or Eastern

32　　　　　　33　　　　　　34

informants. Central informants, however, gave the name katca'-dalaū katca-mset slema tcūwan, *arrowhead-half arrowhead-sharp string stripe*. Thus are named not only the large triangles and the small ones bordering them, but also the white space between the two which to the Indian mind forms a line called string. The second of these patterns was called by Northern informants datō'ī kata xōltū datī'pka, *design empty both-sides sharp-points*. By Central informants it was called katca'-dalaū ctot, *arrowhead-half band*, and also kaca'icai ctot, *butterfly band*. By Eastern informants the name xaca'icai xaga'-daLaū, *butterfly arrowhead-half*, was given, the name butterfly being applied to the large triangles, arrowhead-half to the smaller ones. The pattern of fig. 34 is composed of two distinct elements, the large triangle called by the Northern, Central, and Eastern Pomo respectively, *empty, arrowhead,* and *butterfly,* and the lines of small rectangular figures along their sides. These last are variously called, according to their size, *ant* and *deer-back* by the Northern and Central Pomo, and *ant* and *potato-forehead* by the Eastern Pomo.

In figs. 35, 36, and 37 are shown typical examples of combinations of the isosceles right triangle with other elements, but in these cases the primary arrangement is that shown in fig. 23. Occasionally these figures occur in bands of from two to four of

these large triangles in width, but more often they cover the entire surface of a basket as is shown in pl. 22, fig. 4, and pl. 16, fig. 6. In fig. 35 is seen a rather unusual arrangement of the secondary triangular figures. They are here so placed that one point of the base touches the side of the large triangle instead of sides of the small and large triangles being parallel to each other. The names obtained for this pattern from Northern informants were datŏ'ī kata mina katcak, *design empty over (or upon) arrowhead,* and katca'k datŏī daten, *arrowhead design passing-along (plural).* By Central informants it was called katca'-dalaū u'ī-balaū kŏwaldakadĕtan, *arrowhead-half eye-half following-on-the outside (plural).* Also the name katca-dalaū malada tcūwan, *arrowhead-half near stripe* was obtained. By informants of the Eastern dialect it was called bicĕ'-tŏ kama dilĕ dai gadil, *deer-stand-in mark arrowhead in-the-middle along running along (plural).*

In fig. 36 a combination of these large triangles with small rectangular figures along their borders is shown. This pattern is called by Northern informants datŏ'ī kata xŏl-*tū* bicĕ'-maŏ bitcūtcai, *design empty on-both-sides deer-back small (plural).* The word small is

36

here introduced for the reason that the row of rectangles to be called deer-back must be considerably larger than the very small ones called ants. These seem, according to the informant's notions, to have been part way between the two. Central informants gave the name katca'-dalaū pcĕ'-meŏ malada kaden, *arrowhead-half, deer-back near follow-up.* Eastern informants gave the name bū-dilĕ xaga ko'nawa gadil, *potato-forehead arrowhead on-both-sides passing-along (plural).* By some the design was called merely *butterfly,* xaca'icai.

Fig. 37 represents a pattern which covers the entire surface of a large burden basket. No name was obtained for this pattern among either the Northern or Eastern Pomo but Central informants gave katca'-dalaū malada slema tcūwan, *arrowhead-half near string stripe.*

37

The element called string in this case is not, as in the pattern represented in fig. 32, the white line adjacent to the large triangle, but the black line at a little distance.

Figs. 38 and 39 show a pattern which is met with occasionally, not only as in fig. 37, which if resolved into the smallest possible elements will be seen to be the same as 39, but also as

parts of other patterns and even occasionally as individual figures
such as are shown here.   No special name seems to have been
given to this design by the Northern Pomo.   The only informants
questioned gave such general names as datō'ī katse datsūtka, *design black datsūtka,* and datoi datapka, *design large-area.* Among
the Central and Eastern Pomo, however, special significance was
attached to the lines bordering the triangle in each case.   By the
former the entire design was called katca'-dalaū tū ka'mtiltalī-uī-

kū wī, *arrowhead-half side killdeer-eyebrow.*   The explanation
given by one informant was that the narrow line along the side
of the triangle represented the narrow line above the eye of the
killdeer.   By Eastern informants designs of this kind were called
xaca'icai tsawal-mīsak, *butterfly sunfish-rib.*   Here, as in other
instances, the change of the name of the large isosceles right
triangle from arrowhead among the Northern and Central Pomo
to butterfly among the Eastern is noteworthy.   The angular line
about the triangle is the element called sunfish-rib.   The regular
sunfish-rib design is seen in fig. 225.   These designs were, however, called by one informant kalū'tūduk xacaicai, *striped-watersnake butterfly.*   The fact that the lines about the triangle in
this case meet in an angle was evidently neglected by this informant, who gave them the name commonly applied to any
straight line, such for instance as is shown in fig. 122 or 127.

A very few instances have been noted of a pattern such as is
seen in fig. 40.   By a Northern informant this pattern was called

simply *design sharp,* datoi ditī'p.   By
Central and Eastern informants more descriptive names were given.   By the former it was called tsīyō'tsīyō lala kalū'tcū-
wak, *zigzag in-the-middle blank stripe,* and
by the latter xaga'-datīp dilē kalū'tūduk, *arrowhead-sharp-point
in-the-middle striped-watersnake.*   It will be noted that in the
former case the entire pattern is conceived as a zigzag the same

as though no break occurred through its middle, while in the latter the two halves of the pattern are thought of as separated, sharp pointed arrowheads. Here also the white stripe in the middle is considered by the Central informant not as the striped-watersnake element, but simply as a white or blank stripe. In the majority of cases all informants named only the colored portion of a design, and consequently the term striped-watersnake is most often applied to a straight colored line. This applies to the informants of all three dialectic divisions. Also the white stripe or line such as is shown here is sometimes named striped-watersnake not only by Eastern informants, as in this case, but by others as well.

A single instance was found of the rather peculiar combination of triangular elements such as are shown in fig. 41. Northern informants spoke of this pattern simply as *pointed broad-band,* ditī'pka datsai-banem. A Central informant called it tsīyō'tīyō balaū-ai *ctot, zigzag half (plural) band.* No interpretation was obtained for it among the Eastern Pomo.

Only one instance has been found of the design shown in fig. 42. Northern informants called this datīpka dilē datapka, *sharp points in-the-middle large-area,* by which it is evidently intended to note the wide white stripe through the middle of what would otherwise be a completed figure consisting of two large superimposed isosceles triangles. By Central informants this pattern was called simply *turtle-neck,* kawī'na-ūtca. By one informant also it was spoken of as simply *arrowhead,* thus in both names no mention is made of the white stripe in the middle. Eastern informants called it xaLū xo'nawa xaga gadil kama, *blank on-both-sides arrowheads passing-along (plural) mark.*

The following twelve figs., 43-54, except 53, have to do with triangles whose apexes are acute angles. Figs. 43 and 44 show a design element which occurs occasionally and which is called by Northern informants *arrowhead-sharp,* katca'-miset, or *arrow-*

*head sharp-points,* katca kase'tka. Central informants called it
both *arrowhead-sharp* and *arrowhead-slender,* katca'-mset and
katca'-mtil. By one of the same informants it was, however,
upon one occasion called *zigzag-half,* tsīyŏtsīyō-balaū. By Eastern informants it was called *arrowhead-sharp-pointed* and *arrowhead-projecting* xaga'-datīp and xaga-dīset.

In almost all cases where triangles of any kind are arranged
in rows so that the apexes of one row touch the bases of the row
next above, they do so at the ends of the bases and not in the
middle. Only a single case (fig. 45) has so far been found of the
latter. No special name is given for this pattern, it being considered simply a repetition of that of figure 44.

In the main Pomo design elements are combined to form complex patterns, but upon rare occasions a single triangle or other

element is found placed alone. A few cases of a single sharp
pointed triangle (fig. 46), or having even a sharper point, have
been found. The name *design sharp* or *arrowhead sharp* is usually given for this single element, as well as for those seen in figs.
43-45, where these sharp pointed triangles are combined.

A single case of the odd arrangement of sharp pointed
triangles shown in fig. 47 was found. By some informants this
was simply called a new fashioned or white man's design. By
one Eastern informant, however, it was called *arrowhead-projecting* xaga'-dīset.

In figs. 48-52 are found various combinations of these sharp
pointed triangles with different kinds of large triangles. All these
except that of fig. 49 are of very rare occurrence. The design of
fig. 49, however, is found quite often. In general the names of

all these designs are the same and mentioned the large triangle as well as the small sharp pointed ones set upon its sides. Among the Northern Pomo such figures are called datŏ'ĭ kata xŏltū katca'k daien, *design empty on-both-sides arrowheads collected,* datŏ'ĭ dasĭdasĭka, *design scattered,* or xŏ'ltū katcak, *on-both-sides*

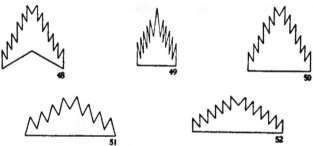

*arrowheads.* By the Central informants these figures are usually spoken of as katca'-dalaū katca-mset, *arrowhead-half arrowhead-sharp,* though they may be called katca'-dalu-mset, *arrowhead-half-sharp,* or the name may even be abbreviated still more to katca'-mset *arrowhead-sharp.* From Eastern informants several different names were obtained, as follows: xaga' hna dīset, *arrowhead and (or with) projecting,* xaga'-daset, *arrowhead-barbed,* xaga-mīset, *arrowhead-sharp,* and kama mīset, *mark sharp.*

The design shown in fig. 53 is a combination of the arrowhead

with the quail plume and the names given it mention both these elements. It is called by Northern and Central informants *quail-plume arrowhead,* cakaga-kēya katcak and caka'ga-kēya katca respectively, and by Eastern informants *arrowhead and (or with) quail-plume,* xaga' na cag'ax-xe.

The design of fig. 54 has been found in but one case. It was

called by a Northern informant *design-sharp,* datŏ'ĭ-ditĭp, by Central informants *arrowhead-sharp,* katca'-mset, and by Eastern informants simply *arrowhead,* xaga'. This is a very unusual and apparently new pattern, though the diagonal line of large isosceles right triangles with many ordinary sharp pointed projections on the lower side of the line is fairly common. Such a pattern is shown in pl. 18, fig. 2.

In fig. 56 is represented one of the typical center designs used in connection with such a complex pattern as that in fig. 55. This design is but rarely found by itself as the pattern of a basket, but frequently occurs in combination with such other elements as

55                    56

compose the pattern of fig. 55, in which case this design takes the place of the zigzag there shown. In this schematic figure the space between the two rows of isosceles triangles has been left blank, making of it merely a white line. In some patterns, however, this space is filled with various other design elements, as for instance a zigzag, or small rectangular figures as is the case in the pattern of the basket shown in pl. 17, fig. 6. Informants named this figure as follows: Northern Pomo, katca'k dilē dakīkītinka, *arrowhead in-the-middle scattered-along-in-a-line*, and datō'ī kata dilē katca'k yo-wil, *design empty in-the-middle arrowheads downward;* Central Pomo, katca'-dalaū tatū tcūwan, *arrowhead-half one (or single) stripe;* and Eastern Pomo, xalū'tūduk hna xagadaset, *striped-watersnake and (or with) arrowheads-barbed.*

57                         58

The interesting lines of isosceles triangles shown in figs. 57 and 58 are called by similar names, notwithstanding the fact that they are arranged in the first case with their points downward and in the second case with their points upward. By Northern informants they were called datō'ī maa mina-datē'kama, *design acorn crossing*, katcak mina-datēkama, *arrowhead crossing*, and datōī datī'pka kana daiyekamū, *design sharp-points close meet (singular).* Central informants called them katca'-mtil ūna'Liū, *arrowhead-slender crossing*, and katca'-dalaū ūna'Liū, *arrowhead-half crossing.* By Eastern informants they were both usually called xaca'icai wīinalīhempke, *butterfly crossing*, or xaca'icai xōldabēhmak, *butterfly meet*. One informant, however, while giving the latter name for fig. 57 gave xaga'-daLaū xōldabēhmak, *arrowhead-half meet*, as the name for fig. 60. It does not appear that the direction in which the triangles point in either of these figures, any more than in other similar cases, such as figures 22-24, establishes whether the design shall be called butterfly or arrowhead-half among the Eastern Pomo.

In figs. 59 and 60 are shown designs which are practically the same, the only real difference being that in the one case the arrangement is horizontal and in the other case diagonal. Only a single example of either of these has as yet been found. They were both called by Northern informants datī'pka dilē masa'-kalak, *sharp-points in-the-middle striped-watersnake*, and by Central informants katca'-mtil ītcai, *arrowhead-slender resemble*. Also by other Central informants the components of these patterns were separately named kawī'na-ūtca, *turtle-neck*, the triangular portion of the figure, and msa'kale, *striped-watersnake*, the line in the middle of the figure, in each case. Eastern informants called these figures xaca'icai dilē gaiya kalū'tūduk, *butterfly in-the-middle gaiya striped-watersnake*. This design in its diagonal arrangement is shown in pl. 17, fig. 2.

An unusual arrangement of triangular elements seen in fig. 61 has been found in one case as the central portion of a band of large triangles, such as those in fig. 25. This design was called by some informants simply *arrowhead*, and by others new or *white man's design*.

Also used as the central part of a band of large triangles, the design shown in fig. 62 has been found, though its use is not at all common. The names obtained for this were simply *arrowhead*, except among the Central Pomo, where *arrowhead-slender*, katca'-mtil, was mentioned by one informant.

An unusual arrangement of triangular figures, seen in fig. 63, was found upon one large boat-shaped basket. This was called in most cases simply arrowhead, though arrowhead-barbed, katca'-daset, and arrowhead-sharp-pointed, xaga'-datīp, were obtained among the Northern and Eastern Pome respectively, and arrowhead-half, katca'-dalaū and xaga-daLaū, among the Central and Eastern Pomo. One Eastern informant also called it *butterfly*, xaca'icai.

### Rectangular Elements.

The Pomo have a variety of four-sided figures, particularly rectangles. Upon the majority of twined baskets and upon many coiled there is found about the border of the opening a band consisting of a repeated rectangular figure. This is the case not only upon baskets whose general design arrangement is banded or horizontal, but also upon baskets the design arrangement of which is any one of the several employed by the Pomo. These rectangular designs are usually arranged in a single row immediately about the border of a basket, and may vary greatly in size, proportions, and arrangement. Figs. 64-72 give practically all the various forms of these bands of single rectangular figures. The general name applied to all these is *finishing design*, rendered by the Northern and Central Pomo baiya'kaū and by the Eastern Pomo hī'baiyax. A second term, hamaka'm, is also found among the Northern Pomo. On account of the prevalence among the whites of the impression that designs of this kind, particularly when made up of small squares, have to do in some way with a fish net, informants were especially questioned upon this subject, and maintained that none of the three terms given have any connection with a fish net. On the other hand they insist that the names mean simply finishing design. In speaking of baiya'kaū informants maintained that the term is not only used to designate the design which finishes or completes a basket, but is a general term used in speaking of any completed piece of work, as, for instance, the finishing of a house or a boat. Among the Central Pomo the design shown in fig. 71 received the name baiya′kaū kam*tilt*ili-ūī-kūwī, *finishing design killdeer's-eyebrow*, on account of the presence of two comparatively small vertical figures or lines at the ends of the large rectangular figures. No such distinction however was made by informants of the other two dialects. Of these several designs the one seen in fig. 64 is by far

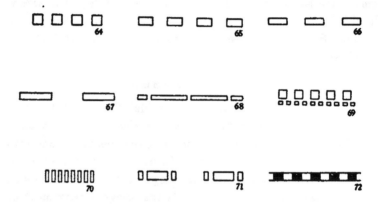

the most common. The designs shown in figs. 65 and 66 are met with quite frequently, but those of much greater length (figs. 67, 68) are rarely found except as worked into the hoop binding of mortar and burden baskets. The design shown in fig. 69 has been found only once, and that in fig. 70 but once as a border finish design. Also only a single example of a border finish design such as that in fig. 72 has been found.

Certain of the above mentioned elements are found not only as finishing designs at the borders of the openings of baskets, but also in bands on the body of the basket itself. These are the designs shown in figures 64, 65, 66, 67, 70, and 72. By the Northern Pomo these designs are usually called dapō′kka, or *large-spots*. The name bicē′-o, *deer-teeth*, is also used. These elements are, however, different from the ordinary deer-tooth design (fig. 74). Central informants usually spoke of these designs as *deer-back*, pcē′-meō, though when very small that of fig. 64 was also called *ants, tūn'tūn.* In addition to these two names certain informants spoke of them as *finishing designs,* giving the same name as if they had been placed upon the border of the basket, and stating that they were intended to be the same figures as those about the border. In the case of the design of figure 70, which occurred several times in the bodies of baskets, all the Central informants questioned gave it the name *finishing design,* baiya'-kaū. Eastern informants called these designs in most cases *potato-forehead,* bū'-dilē. These are not, however, the ordinary potato-forehead designs of the Eastern dialect, which are shown in figs. 80 and 95. By one Eastern informant the design of fig. 64 was called *deer-teeth,* bicĕ'-yaŏ.

In speaking of the finishing design it should also be noted that these same designs, as well as those of several other kinds, notably zigzags, such as that in fig. 139, are found quite commonly as the first or *inital design* upon the bottom of a basket, whether the design arrangement is horizontal, spiral, or diagonal. In such cases informants usually gave these designs, regardless of their form, a name which is best rendered by the term *initial design.* The various designs used initially are called caiyŏ'ī by the Pomo of all three divisions. The word appears to have certain other meanings, as follows: wedding or other presents made by one person to another. It does not apply, however, to the return present of equal value made, according to Pomo custom, by the second party to the first. The term is also applied to a prayer or wish for good luck, to the feast given to secure recovery from illness, and to beads thrown upon the dancing floor during a ceremony. The idea of a prayer or wish for god luck seems to be related to its use as the name of this initial design upon baskets; for some, at least, of the Indians believe that if the maker, especially of a twined basket, omits this design blindness will be the result, a belief very closely related to that connected with the dau or opening in horizontal or banded patterns.

A single example of a rectangular design such as that in fig. 73 has been found. Designs of such rather unusual kinds are ordinarily spoken of as *new,* new style, new fashioned, or white mans' designs. One Central informant, however, spoke of this figure as pcĕ'-meŏ tatū, *deer-back one (or single).*

Square or other variously proportioned rectangles arranged in patterns of two or more rows are frequently found.  One of the most commonly occurring designs is that shown in fig. 74, where a double row of very small squares or rectangles is placed horizontally in a band about a basket, or is used as the design for filling the space between the rows of large triangular figures in

73                              74

spiral patterns.  The former is the more common use.  Its position in relation to the opening of a basket governs, to a certain extent, its name, as in the case of a single row of squares or rectangles.  If used as a border about the opening of a basket, it is almost always called simply *finishing design*, baiya′kaŭ, or hamaka′m by the Northern, baiya′kaŭ by the Central, and hī′-baiyax by the Eastern Pomo.  By some informants this was given the same name when used as a border about the opening of a basket or placed farther down in the body.  In the latter position it is called by the Northern Pomo, bitū′mtū datōī, *ant design,* though it is also sometimes called, dapō′kka, *large-spots* or dapō′dapōka, *spotted.*  Another name is *deer-teeth,* bicē-o, and one informant also called it *mosquito design,* bita′mta datōī. Central informants usually called it *tū′ntūn, ants,* if made up of very small rectangles, and *deer-back,* pcē-meō, if made up of larger rectangles.  Eastern informants, however, gave more frequently *deer-teeth,* bicē′-yao, though *tūntūn, ants* was also used.  When the rectangles are very small, ant design is almost always the name applied to this design by the people speaking each dialect. Deer-teeth implies a design composed of larger rectangular, usually square, figures.  Spots or large spots is more usually applied to a design consisting of comparatively large rectangular figures particularly if they are placed at considerable distances from one another, though these names are not so used extensively in any case.

Small squares or rectangles arranged in patterns consisting of more than two rows as shown in figs. 75 and 76 are quite frequently met with.  In the main all informants questioned named these two figures the same. The Northern Pomo called them *ant design,* bitŭ'mtŭ datōī. By one Northern informant was added the qualifying term datsa'i-banem, signifying *broad-band.* Central informants called these designs tŭ'ntŭn tcī or *tŭn'tŭn,*

75                                              76

*ctot, ant design or ant band.* Eastern informants called them bicē'-yao, *deer-teeth,* bicē'-yao kŭt, *deer-teeth small,* and tŭntŭn, *ants.* In the case of the design shown in fig. 76, however, some informants noted the presence of the lines bordering the band of small rectangular figures. By one Central informant the name msa'kale, *striped-watersnake* was given, and by one Eastern informant, kalŭ'tŭduk na xam bŭ-dile, *striped-watersnake and (or with) among potato-forehead.*

A few cases of a design consisting of rectangles such as those in fig. 77 have been found. This design was called by Northern Pomo informants datōī dapō'kka datsa'i-banem, *design large-spots broad-band.* By Central informants it was called *deer-back,* pcē'-meō, to which the word *band, ctot,* was added by certain of them since this design occurs only in a horizontal or banded arrangement. Eastern informants gave this design the name bŭ'-dilē kō'nawa kalŭ'tŭduk, *potato-forehead on-both-sides striped-watersnake.* Some called it simply *potato-forehead,* taking no account of the presence of the two lines on the sides. By one informant it was called tŭ'ntŭn tīa, *ants big.* In this last name appears a practice which is met with quite frequently and which shows the prevalence of modifying terms in Pomo design names. Here the word big is added to the name of the design for the reason that the rectangles are in this case considerably larger than those in the regular designs called ants, such for instance, as is shown in fig. 75. In the same manner, a line of small rectangles (fig. 74) and which would ordinarily be spoken of by some informants as ants, might be called by others deer-back small or potato-forehead small, they

77

being smaller than the rectangles ordinarily referred to by the
names deer-back and potato-forehead.

One instance of a rectangular design such as is shown in fig.
78 has been found. Northern Pomo infor-
mant called this design bicĕ'-maō dilē dakĭ-
kĭtin, *deer-back in-the-middle scattered
along*. Central informants called it simply
*deer-back* or *deer-back band*, pcĕ'-meō or

pcĕ'-meō ctot. A name for the design was obtained from but one
Eastern informant who called it La'l-a-pa, *goose-excrement*. This,
however, is not the design ordinarily referred to as goose excrement by Eastern informants. That design is composed of
parallelograms whose angles are other than right angles, such, for
instance, as those shown in figs. 103 and 105.

Another rectangular design found upon only one basket is
that shown in fig. 79. By Northern Pomo informants, this was
called *deer-back broad-band*, bicĕ'maō datsai-banem or simply
*deer-back*, bicĕ'-maō. Central informants called it *deer-back
band*, pcĕ'-meō ctot, or simply *deer-back*, pcĕ-meō. The name
given it by Eastern informants was *potato-forehead* or *potato-
forehead big*, bū'-dilē or bū-dilē tĭa.

The design seen in fig. 80 occurs very frequently, in fact, almost as frequently as that of fig. 74. The lengths of these rectangles vary, and the particular rectangles here shown are only
typical of the variously proportioned ones which are considerably longer than they are broad. They all bear the same names.
This double row of long rectangles arranged horizontally is most
frequently called by the Northern Pomo bicĕ'maō, *deer-back*,
though it is also frequently spoken of as *large-spots* dapō'kka.
The name *deer-back*, pcĕ'-meō, was uniformly obtained from Central Pomo informants, while bū'-dilē, *potato-forehead*, was the
name usually obtained from Eastern informants. To this name
xōtcagan, *running-along-in-pairs*, was also added by one inform-

ant, in the case of one of the many examples of this design. By another Eastern informant this design was called bicĕ'-tō kama, *deer-stand-in mark.*

Designs consisting of two or more rows of long rectangles,

such as those shown in figs. 81 and 82, are occasionally met with. Northern Pomo informants called these *deer-back design,* bicĕ'-maō datōī, or *large-spots,* dapō'kka. Central and Eastern informants gave respectively the names *deer-back* and *potato-fore-head,* pcĕ'-meō and bū'-dilē to both designs. In the case of the design shown in fig. 81, one Central informant added cte'ltele, which signifies *hitched-together or connected,* to the ordinary term deer-back.

One case of the combined line and rectangle design or, more strictly speaking, pattern (fig. 83) was noted. Northern Pomo informants called this mīsa'kalak xōltū dapō'kka tcacītemūl, *striped-watersnake on-both-sides large spots going-around-and-meeting (plural).* Central informants called it pcĕ'-meō tcī ta-kanma tcīltaū, *deer-back design far-apart stuck-on.* Eastern informants gave the name bū'-dilē xam xalū'tūduk, *potato-forehead among striped-watersnake.*

In fig. 84 is represented a design based primarily upon rectangular figures, arranged in two bands about a large globose plain twined cooking basket. By one Eastern informant this design was called simply *ant mark,* tū'ntūn kama. By Northern Pomo informants, however, the more descriptive term, bitū'mtū dilē masa'kalak, *ants in-the-middle striped-watersnake* was given. By one Central informant *ant mark,* tūntūn kama, was given as the name of this design, but by others *finishing-design band,* bai-ya'kaū ctot, or the more descriptive name, *finishing-design string in-the-middle stripe,* baiya'kaū slema lala tcūwan, was given.

A single case of a rectangular design such as that in fig. 85 was found. Northern Pomo informants called this dapŏ'kka dilē cĭke'tka, *large spots in-the-middle stripe.* By one informant also it was called maa-ka'tōla datōi, said to signify *acorn-cup design.* Central informants called it pcĕ'-meō tatū, *deer-back one (or single),* though baiya'kaū, *finishing-design,* was given in one case. From Eastern informants bū'-dilē, *potato-forehead,* and bū'dile xalĭ, *potato-forehead one (or single),* as well as bicĕ'-yaō, deer-teeth, were obtained as names.

In fig. 86 is seen an unusual rectangular design and one of rare occurrence. Its Northern Pomo name is bicĕ'-maō dilē daki'tka, *deer-back in-the-middle scattered-around.* Also batcō'tama dĭka'tka, *one-on-top-of-another pushed-over* was given as its name by another informant. By most Central informants it was called *deer-back band,* pcĕ'-meō ctot, though by one it was called simply *white man's design,* masa'n tcĭ, meaning that it was not an aboriginal pattern. Its Eastern name is *deer-back mark,* bicĕ'-maō kama.

Fig. 87 shows a pattern found in only one instance. By Northern informants it was called daki'tka, *scattered-around* by Central informants pcĕ'-meō ctot, *deer-back band,* or pcĕ'-meō base't ctot, *deer-back ugly (or imperfect) band.* Its Eastern dialect name is bicĕ'-yaō, *deer-teeth.*

The rectangular design represented in fig. 88 is found occasionally as a separate pattern worked in a colored fiber material on the surface of the basket (pl. 21, fig. 3), or it may be worked in white material in the center of a larger figure made of colored fibers, as, for instance, a large triangular figure. In such a case, the portion of the design appearing in this schematic figure in black is, of course, white. The names given to this design are as follows: by the Northern and Central Pomo, *deer-back,* bicĕ'maŏ and pcĕ'-meŏ respectively: by the Central Pomo, the modifying terms tcadōtcadō tcil, *circular stuck-on,* were added to pcĕ'-meŏ in one case, and the term ptcŏ'yai, *short (plural),* was added upon another occasion. By the Eastern Pomo the design was called bū'-dilĕ or bū'-dilĕ winalĭhempke, *potato-forehead* or *potato-forehead crossing.*

89

90

What may be called the negative of the design shown in fig. 88 is found in fig. 89. In all three of the Pomo divisions it is called *deer-back.* From the Eastern Pomo the name *potato-forehead* was also obtained. This figure is of very rare occurrence.

Diamond shaped or square patterns (fig. 90) consisting of small rectangles are occasionally found. One Northern informant called this pattern dapō'dapō, *spotted,* referring to the whole mass of small rectangles as a unit. Central informants spoke of it simply as *deer-back,* pcĕ'meŏ, and Eastern informants called it *potato-forehead,* bū'-dilĕ.

91

92

Rectangular designs of slightly more frequent occurrence are those in figs. 91 and 92. Here, as in other cases where designs consisting of small squares or rectangles are concerned, the size of the component rectangles governs the name. To both these patterns Northern informants applied the names dapō'kka, *large-spots,* bicĕ'-maŏ, *deer-back,* and bitū'mtū, ants, according as the size of the rectangles varied from large to small. In the Central dialect pcĕ'-meŏ, *deer-back,* was the only elemental name obtained for either of these figures, though various qualifying terms, such as tcī'ltaū, *stuck on (plural),* ptcŏ'yai, *short (plural),* and katsu't-tciū, *swelled,* were used by different informants. By the Eastern Pomo, a distinction similar to that among the Northern is made.

A design of large rectangles is called bū'-dilē, *potato-forehead*, and one of small rectangles, *tū'ntūn, ants.*

Small rectangles, arranged in the form of a zigzag as shown in fig. 93, are occasionally found. The fact of the zigzag arrangement of these elements seems not to have impressed the informants in this case, though in the design seen in fig. 94, which is practically identical with that in fig. 93 except that double instead

93

94

of single rows of rectangles are used, they made mention of the zigzag arrangement in almost all cases. In the case of the design shown in fig. 93, the simple name *deer-back*, among the Northern Pomo bicē'-maŏ, and among the Central Pomo pcē'-meŏ, was given, while the name given by the Eastern Pomo was *ants*, *tū'ntūn*. In the case of the design shown in fig. 94 similar names, but with zigzag added, were given. By Northern informants it was called bitū'mtū tsīyŏtsīyŏka, *ants zigzag*. By Central informants it was called pcē'-meŏ tsīyŏtsīyŏ, *deer-back zigzag*. Eastern informants differentiated the patterns according to the size of the rectangles comprising them, calling the comparatively large rectangles bū'-dilē dzīyŏ'dzīyŏ, *potato-forehead zigzag*, and the small ones tū'ntūn dzīyŏdzīyŏ, *ants zigzag.*

One of the more commonly occurring designs composed of rectangles is that shown in fig. 95. This design often occurs alone

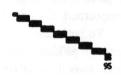
95

as a pattern covering the entire surface of a basket. The diagonal rows of rectangles are placed with more or less space between them. In such cases, the design is almost always called by the Northern and Central Pomo *deer-back*, bicē'-maŏ and pcē-meŏ respectively. By the Eastern Pomo it is called *potato-forehead*, bū'-dilē. In case, however, the component rectangles are comparatively small, the name given to this design by informants of all three divisions was *ants*, bitū'mtū in the Northern, and tū'ttūn in both the Central and Eastern. In addition to its use alone as a pattern proper, it is also frequently used as one of the constituent elements of a complex pattern. Instances of this are found in figs. 34 and 36 which, however, do not occur so frequently as patterns similar to that shown in fig. 55 in which a diagonal line of rectangles runs through the middle of the pattern in the place here occupied by the zigzag. Instances of such patterns occur on the baskets of pl. 18, figs. 5, 6, and pl. 19, fig. 3. The names given it under these circumstances in the different dialects are the same as those used when it is employed alone as a pattern. It is noticeable, however, that when employed thus, it is more frequently called deer-back or potato-forehead, probably due as much to the fact that the other figures composing the design are compara-

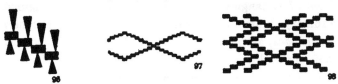

tively larger than these rectangles as that they themselves are actually very small. In one of the cases above mentioned, that shown in fig. 36, the pattern is named by the Northern Pomo datō'ī kata xōltū bicē'-maō bitcūtcai, *design empty on-both-sides deer-back small (plural)* or datō'ī kata xōltū bitūmtū datōī, *design empty on-both-sides ants design.* These differences in name are due, as before stated, to the differences in size of the rectangles, though the same figure may be named deer-back by one informant and ants by another, according to the informant's personal conceptions of these particular elements of the pattern and according as their relative sizes differ. Similar descriptive names in which the rectangular element of the design is mentioned are given by the Central and Eastern Pomo, who call it respectively katca'-dalaū pcē-meō malada tcūwan, *arrowhead-half deer-back near stripe,* and bū'dilē xaga kō'nawa gadil, *potato-forehead arrowhead on-both-sides passing-along (plural).*

Another example of this design combined with a different element is shown in fig. 96, in which the rectangular part is the principal element instead of one of the subordinate elements as is most generally the case. Only one example of this pattern has as yet been found. It was called by Northern and Central Pomo informants *deer-back*, but one Northern informant gave as its full name bicĕ'-maŏ tū ditī'pka, *deer-back side pointed*.

In figs. 97 and 98 are shown designs consisting of single and double rows respectively of rectangles so arranged that the rows cross each other. The names in both these cases are the same, no account being taken of the fact that one consists of single and the other of double rows of rectangles. They are called by the Northern Pomo bitū'mtū datōī mina-date'kamū, *ant design crossing*, and bicĕ'-maŏ mina-date'kamū, *deer-back crossing*. By the Central Pomo they are called pcĕ'-meŏ ūnaLiū, *deer-back crossing*, and by the Eastern Pomo bū'-dilē wīna'līhempke, *potato-forehead crossing*, and tū'ntūn wīnalīhempke, *ants crossing*. In crossing, these lines of rectangles form hollow diamond shaped figures. The ordinary figure of this shape is called by the Northern Pomo *turtle-back*, kawī'na-tcīdik and by the Central Pomo *acorn-head*, pdū'-cna and it is an interesting fact that some informants make compound names out of deer-back or ants and turtle-back or acorn-head as, for instance, pcĕ-meŏ pdū'cna, *deer-back acorn-cup*, thus not only naming the lines of rectangles which constitute the elements of the pattern, but also mentioning the large figures which these lines form.

One case of a design composed of lines of hollow rectangles so arranged that they cross each other (fig. 99) was found. Two

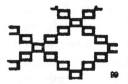

Northern Pomo informants gave the name kawī'na-tcīdik, *turtle-back*, but this probably referred to the large hollow diamond shaped figure formed by the crossing lines rather than to the small hollow rectangles themselves. One Eastern informant gave to this design the name xaitsa'kai kama, which may be roughly rendered, *stretcher design*.[*]

### Rhomboidal Elements.

Quite common among Pomo designs are rhomboidal figures. These may be variously arranged in single rows or in patterns from two to four rows in width. The proportions of the length and breadth of these rhomboidal figures vary greatly,

----

[*] The term stretcher as used here is explained above in the discussion of the design in fig. 15.

as do also their angles.   The various forms in which these rhomboids occur are shown in figs. 100 to 113.   Since these designs stand mid-way between those composed of the rectangular figures just treated, and the zigzag designs such as 148, etc., and since they vary considerably in form and arrangement, there are considerable differences in the names given them.   By Northern informants the rhomboidal design shown in fig. 100 was called

*deer-back*, bicĕ'-maŏ, *sharp-points*, datī'pka, and *zigzag*, tsīyŏ'tsīyŏ.   By Central informants it was called *crow-foot (or track)*, kaa'i-kama, *deer-back*, pcĕ'-meŏ, and *zigzag*, ka'tīyŏtīŏ.   By Eastern informants it was called bicĕ'-tŏ, *deer-stand in*.   The connection is not very clear and no satisfactory explanation could be obtained from the Indians as to this last name.   It was also called xatī'yo'tī'yŏ, *zigzag*, xaga'-dīset, *arrowheads-projecting*, and dītīp, *sharp*.

The design shown in fig. 101, which differs from that of fig. 100 only in having a heavy line bordering the lower side of the double row of rhomboidal figures, was called by Northern

Pomo informants datī'pka datsa'ibanem, *sharp-points broad-band*, also by one informant, bicĕ'-maŏ, *deer-back*.   It should be remembered, however, that the regular deer-back design is composed of rectangles and it is probable that this informant did not here, as in the case of the design shown in fig. 100, differentiate between the rectangles and the rhomboidal figures.   Central and Eastern informants gave respectively the names kaa'i-kama, *crow-foot (or track)* and bicĕ-to ku'ta, *deer-stand-in-small*.   But one instance was found of this particular design.

The design shown in fig. 102 was found upon two baskets. It differs from the last mentioned only in having a line on each side instead of on but one side of the double row of rhomboidal figures.   The names bicĕ'-maŏ datsaibanem, *deer-back broad-band* and ka'tsīyŏtsīyŏ, *zig-zag*, were given by Northern informants to this design. Central informants all called it kaa'i-kama, *crow-foot (or track)*.   Greater differences are found, however, in the names given it by Eastern informants. It was called xaīī'yoīī'yō, *zigzag,* bicē'maō, *deer-back,* bū-dilē tsīyō'tsīyō, *potato-forehead zigzag,* and cō bax kama, *east this mark,* commonly spoken of as a "design from the east." One informant who frequently used this term maintained that the patterns to which she applied it were actually extraneous ones, introduced to the Eastern Pomo from the people living to the east of them. Other informants, however, claimed that these designs were original with the Pomo and that this name did not imply that they were introduced from any other people.

103

104

One example of a design consisting of a quadruple row of long rhomboidal figures such as that in fig. 103 has been found. One name obtained for this design among the Northern Pomo was bicē'-maō, datsa'ibanem, *deer-back broad-band.* It was called kaa'i-kama, *crow-foot (or track),* and kaa'i-kama kōlai, *crow-foot (or track) long (plural)* by Central informants, and Lal-a-pa, *goose-excrement,* by Eastern informants.

Only one example has been found of a design consisting of a quadruple row of very small rhomboidal figures, such as that in fig. 104. This was called by the Northern Pomo katcak datsa'i-banem, *arrowhead broad-band.* By Central informants it was called kaa'i-kama, *crow-foot (or track),* and pdū'-cna, *acorn-head (or cup).* The one name obtained for it in the Eastern dialect was bicē'-maō, *deer-back.*

A design consisting of long rhomboidal figures but so arranged that they slant toward the left instead of toward the right (fig. 105) is occasionally found. This is called by the Northern Pomo

105

sometimes dītī'pka datsaibanem, *pointed broad-band,* though they are also called bicē'-maō, *deer-back,* bicē'-yeē-nat, *deer-breast-?,* and datcē'kka, said to be the name of *a game* in which a long wooden or other skewer is thrust through as many as possible of a string of fish vertebrae as the string is passing through the air. Central informants called it kaa'i-kama, *crow-foot (or track).* Eastern informants most often called it xatī''yō'tī'yō, *zigzag,* though here again the name cō'bax kama, *east this mark,* appears.

106

107

Examples of double or triple rows of these rhomboids (figs. 106 and 107) pointing toward the left and bordered by heavy lines have been found, although they are of very rare occurrence. They are called by the Northern Pomo *zigzag,* ka'tīyōtīyō, and *deer-back,* bicĕ'-maō. By the Eastern Pomo they are called either *zigzag,* xatī'yō'tī'yō, or *east this mark,* oō' bax kama, and by the Central Pomo they are called *crow-foot (or track),* kaa'i-kama.

The white rhomboidal design shown in fig. 108 was called by the Northern Pomo informants datsa'ibanem dīlē datī'pka, *broad-band in-the-middle sharp-points.* By Central informants it was called kaa'i-kama, *crow-foot (or track),* and by Eastern in-

108

formants bū'-dilē xalī, *potato-forehead one (or single),* and xaitsa'k na xal'ū'tūduk kadabemlī, *stretcher and (or with) striped-watersnake going-around (plural).* This design is of very rare occurrence.

109

110

One case each of a white rhomboidal design (fig. 109) and of a colored rhomboidal design (fig. 110) have been found. These are usually called simply zigzag by the people of the three Pomo divisions under consideration, though among the Northern Pomo the name datī'p dīlē katca'k kale cīden, *sharp-point in-the-middle arrowhead white lead,* was obtained for the design shown in fig. 109. It is evident that the informant in this case took into account not only the white figures, which, to the minds of the other informants, constituted a zigzag, but also the dark sharp pointed portion of the pattern as well.

111

112

The unusual arrangements of rhomboidal figures such as appear in figs. 111 and 112 were found upon the same basket. The former was called by Northern informants bicē'-maŏ datsa'iba-nem, *deer-back broad-band*. Both were called by Eastern informants La'l-a-pa hna xalū' cūdil kama, *goose-excrement (or with) blank lead mark,* and cō' bax kama, *east this mark.* Central informants claimed that both these patterns were new and had no regular Indian name, being simply called new fashioned or *white man's design,* masa'n tcī. The design of fig. 112 was called by Northern informants bicē'-maŏ datōī dilē kale cīde'n, *deer-back design in-the-middle white lead.*

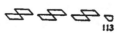
113

114

The design consisting of a pair of parallelograms placed so that two of their oblique angled corners touch (fig. 113) has been found on a very few baskets. This was called by Northern Pomo informants datoi datipka, *design sharp-points,* and bicē'-maŏ datōi, *deer-back design.* By Central informants it was called kaa'i-kama, *crow-foot,* and ka'tīyotīyō, *zigzag,* and by Eastern informants usually dzīyōdzīyō or xatī'yotī'yo, *zigzag.* Another Eastern informant gave the name xama ditīp, *mark sharp.*

A single example was found of a design like that in fig. 114. This was claimed by some informants to be a new fashioned or *white man's design.* No Indian name was given by any of them for it.

### Linear Elements.

The designs shown in the six figures 115 to 120 are what may be termed intermediate forms between angular figures of considerable length and true linear figures. Patterns of this kind

occur very rarely, one example only of each of these having thus
far been noted. They are often called by informants new-
fashioned or *white man's designs*, and, when given true Indian
names, are usually called *striped* or *striped-watersnake*. In the
case of the design shown in fig. 118, however, more descriptive

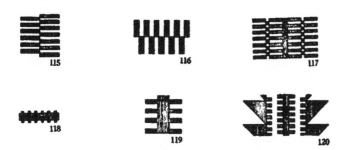

terms are employed by Northern and Eastern informants who
respectively call this design mīsa'kalak xōl*t*ū katca'k, *striped-
watersnake on-both-sides arrowheads*, and kalū'tūduk hna bicē-
yaō, *striped-watersnake and (or with) deer-teeth*. The design
shown in fig. 120 was called by Eastern informants xaga' dilē
gaiya gadil xa'itsakai kama, *arrowheads in-the-middle gaiya
passing-along (plural) stretcher mark*.

Simple lines arranged in such a manner that they cross each
other (fig. 121) and form squares or diamond shaped figures are

occasionally found, but it happens more
frequently that these crossing lines are met
with in an elaborate crossing pattern where
they are in combination with other design
elements. When found thus alone, they
are sometimes called simply *crossing*. An example of one of
these simple crossing line patterns was called by the Northern
Pomo wina-da*t*ē'kama, crossing or literally *top-lie-on*, by the
Central Pomo ūna'Liū, *crossing*, and by the Eastern Pomo wīna-
līhe'mpke, which has the same signification. In another case
(fig. 233) which consists of crossing rows of a pattern formed
from the triangular elements shown in figs. 17, 18, 19, and 20,
the central space between the lines of triangles is left blank,
thus making a set of crossing white lines. This pattern was

called by Northern informants *arrowheads crossing*, katcaʹk mina-datēkama, and *arrowhead in-the-middle scattered-along-in-a-line*, katcaʹk dile dakĭkīti′nka.  By Central informants it was called katca′-mtil ūnaLiū, *arrowhead-slender crossing*.  By Eastern informants the name given was xalū′tūduk hna xaga′-daset wĭnalĭ-hempke, *striped-watersnake and (or with) arrowheads-barbed crossing.*

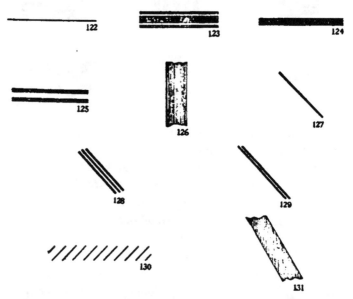

Straight lines of varying widths are frequently found on Pomo baskets.  These may be arranged horizontally, diagonally, or vertically and may be placed so that two or three parallel lines form a broad pattern unit, as well as so that each line stands by itself.  Examples of various arrangements of single or parallel lines of varying widths are shown in figs. 122 to 131.  When used by themselves as patterns, these single or parallel linear figures are usually called *striped-watersnake* by all informants. Among the Northern Pomo the most common form of this name is mīsa′kalak, though mĭsa′kala and masakalak are frequently found.  Among the Central Pomo the name is the same with phonetic variations, msa′kale.  Among the Eastern Pomo, however, this snake has an entirely different name, kalū′tūduk and kalŭ′tŭruk, of which the former is the more common. In addition to their independent use as the entire pattern of the basket, these linear figures are found very frequently in combination with other design elements, particularly in the complex diagonally arranged triangular patterns, which are so prominent on some forms of Pomo baskets. They may appear as lines of color through the center of one of these complex patterns, as is the case in pl. 22, fig. 5, or as white lines in this same position (pl. 28, fig. 1). In either case, particularly in the former, they are called striped-watersnake. In the latter case, however, they are not infrequently called by the Central Pomo *string*, sle′ma or sle′mat. Obviously, only the diagonal lines can be employed in the complex triangle patterns above mentioned and in these cases more than three parallel lines have not as yet been found, grouped together. A single line in the middle of one of these complex patterns is quite common. So far, no complex pattern horizontally arranged has been found containing either colored or white straight lines in its middle. It appears to make no difference whether there be one, two, or three lines arranged together, the names given are the same. The most commonly occurring of these designs are the single narrow horizontal line (fig. 122) and the single narrow diagonal line (fig. 127), the former being met with very frequently as a pattern in full, the latter almost as frequently as one of the elements of a complex pattern. The broader single lines in both these arrangements (figs. 124 and 131) are found only occasionally. A pattern consisting of a double narrow horizontal line (fig. 125) is found quite often. The remainder of the various linear designs above referred to, figs. 123, 126, 128, 129, and 130 are of comparatively rare occurrence.

In the cases of very broad linear designs such as those shown in figs. 126 and 131, other names than striped-watersnake are sometimes given. In the case of fig. 126, some Northern informants gave the name data′pka, signifying *a large area*, while one Central informant called it katca′k-kalatkaŭ, *arrowhead-drawn-out,* and an Eastern informant gave xaga′datap, *arrowhead-large-area.* The reason for the conception of this figure as a long pointed arrowhead is most likely to be found in the fact that the design is worked vertically upon a curved surface, which naturally tends to cause it to narrow and approach more or less nearly a point at either end. Other informants, however, considered it simply a broad line. In the case of the design of fig. 131 the name given by one Northern informant was data'pka, *large area.*

The V-shaped design (fig. 132) has been found upon but a few baskets and in these cases was not at all prominent. It was always spoken of by Central informants as *sunfish-rib*, tsawa'l-msak, but it differs materially from the true sunfish-rib design as shown in figs. 224 and 225. Designs such as those shown in figs. 132 and 133 are considered as more or less new and are unnamed by some informants. The design shown in fig. 132 was also called by Northern Pomo informants tsīkē'ga, *zigzag* (?), and datō'ī cīket, *design striped.* By Central informants it was also called ditcī kalat. Ditcī signifies *design or pattern* and kala't is said to be applied to *approximately parallel lines,* such, for instance, as those which might be made by the dragging of two or three objects through the dust, which would result in lines not entirely straight and parallel but approximately so. Eastern informants also called this figure *sunfish-rib*, tsawa'l-mīsak, and *striped-watersnake*, kalū'tūduk. The one case where the design shown in fig. 133 occurred was on a rather coarsely woven basket of three-rod foundation. In such a basket it is obviously impossible to make a diagonal straight line, the nearest approach to this being a succession of small rectangles, each overlapping those nearest and projecting a little farther to the side than the one below. These small rectangular figures are called deer-back by the Northern and Central Pomo, and potato-forehead by the Eastern Pomo. The names given by some informants to these designs were simply *deer-back,* bicĕ'-maō among the Northern Pomo and pcĕ'meō among the Central Pomo, and *potato-forehead,* bū-dilē, among the Eastern Pomo. In addition to these names, however, some of the Eastern informants also gave sun-fish-rib, tsawa'l-mĭsak, thus taking into account the angular nature of the design. As before stated, however, most inform-ants called the designs of both these figures new or *white man's designs*.

The same statement applies to the peculiar linear designs shown in figs. 134 and 135. These designs have been so far found upon a single basket each and were not given Indian names by most informants. The design shown in fig. 134 occurred, in the one case where it was found, as the initial design on the bottom of the basket shown in pl. 19, fig. 1, and informants gave it the name caiyō'i, *initial design*. One Eastern informant also called it bicĕ'-yaō, *deer-teeth*, while another gave its name as caga'x-xe, *quail-plume*. One Central informant called it simply ka'taiītcai, which is said to mean *separated (plural)* (?). As is shown in the illustration, but four of these figures occur in the circle of design, thus making the spaces between them very considerable. This undoubtedly accounts for this general name, which applies not only to this case where the constituents of the pattern are separated by considerable distances but also to all other designs where the distances between component parts are large.

In fig. 136 is shown a *cross* which was universally said by the Indians to be copied from the whites. It is a reproduction upon  the basket of the cross of the Roman Cath-olic church, which has its churches in sev-eral parts of the Pomo country as well as a Franciscan Mission upon the southern shore of Clear lake. By Central inform-ants, most of whom embrace the Catholic faith, this design was called karū's, clearly derived from the Spanish cruz. One East-ern informant called it kama' bana, *mark forked*. This, like most new designs, is found but rarely, and when used it is almost always secondary to the main pattern as is the case upon the basket shown in pl. 18, fig. 6.

An odd design is represented in fig. 137. It was called by Northern informants dasī′dasī-mūl, *scattered-around-in-a-circle*, also datō′ī bīyōbīyōka, *design little-pieces*, and dapō′dapōka, *spotted*. By Central informants it was called tsawa′l-msak, *sunfish-rib*, though tsīyō′tsīyō, *zigzag*, was also given. One Eastern informant called it tsīyō′tsīyō-dīset, *zigzag-projecting*, though

137                     138

most Eastern informants simply called it caiyōī, *initial design*, since in the one case in which it was found it occurred as a circle near the center of the bottom of the basket shown in pl. 16, fig. 6.

One case of the linear design in fig. 138 was also found. By informants of all three Pomo divisions this was called new or *white man's design*, but one Northern informant called it dīka′tka datōī, *pushed-over design*.

### Zigzag Elements.

Among the most frequently occurring Pomo designs are various forms of zigzags. The various forms and arrangements of these zigzags are shown in figs. 139 to 194. Many of these, regardless of whether they are arranged horizontally, vertically, or diagonally and regardless of the thickness of their component lines or of the angles which these lines make with one another, are called simply *zigzag* by the informants of all the three Pomo divisions here considered. The term zigzag, by which the Indians seem to mean almost any crooked line or object, is most commonly rendered by the Northern and Central Pomo tsīyō′tsīyō and by the Eastern Pomo dzīyō′dzīyō. Different individuals, however, vary from these forms so that dzīyōdzīyō is occasionally used by Northern informants, and tsīyō′tsīyō is used by informants of all three divisions. In addition to these variants of the same term, which informants all claimed signify precisely the same thing, there is a term which is virtually the same as the above but preceded by ka or xa. Additional forms of these terms are therefore ka′tsīyōtsīyō, katīyōtīyō, katī′yō′tī′yō, xatīyōtīyō, and xatī′yō′tī′yō. Ka or xa is never added before dzīyō′dzīyō.

Informants seem not to be very clear in their own minds as to
the exact difference, if there is any, between tsīyŏ'tsīyŏ and
its variants, and ka'tíyŏtíyŏ and its variants. Some claim that
the former is a general term applied to almost any kind of
zigzag and that the latter is applied exclusively to the diagonal
zigzag consisting of a horizontal straight line with a neck, or vertical straight line, much smaller and at right angles to the first,
such as that in fig. 170. Others maintain that it is the name of a
diagonal zigzag (fig. 176) in which both the horizontal portion
and the neck are the same width, but the neck is much shorter
than the horizontal portion. Some further restrict the term to
figures of this description, but those in which the horizontal line
and the neck meet each other at acute angles. However, none of
these definitions are adhered to at all strictly in the naming of
designs; some informants even using the latter set of terms as
names for various designs which are not arranged diagonally at
all. Close questioning has thus far failed to discover an exact
and uniform meaning for these names, and it has therefore been
deemed advisable to render both sets of term as *zigzag*. It has
been suggested that ka'tíyŏtíyŏ had reference to rippling water,
the idea no doubt arising from the fact that water is called in the
various Pomo dialects ka or xa, thus easily making *water zigzag*.
The Indians, however, maintain that ka'tíyŏtíyŏ has no connection
whatever with water and that there is no place, as for instance
a riffle, in a stream or any point in a lake which bears this name.
In addition to the above mentioned names for zigzag designs they
are also called by some Northern and Central Pomo informants
tsīyŏ'tsīyŏka and by the Eastern Pomo dzīyŏ'dzīyŏka. Still
another term rendered by Northern informants as zigzag is tsakŏ'-
tsakŏka, and a term of almost the same significance is dikŏ'tka,
which the same people translate as wavy. The term tsīkĕ'ya
probably also signifies zigzag, though no entirely certain and
satisfactory translation has been obtained for it.

A zigzag design of very common occurrence is that shown in
fig. 139. It consists simply of a narrow broken line, the successive parts of which meet each other in right or nearly right angles.
The names given this design are tsīyŏ'tsīyŏ by the Northern and
Central Pomo and dzīyŏdzīyŏ by the Eastern Pomo.

A few cases have been found of what might be termed the negative of the design shown in fig. 139. This design, shown in fig. 140, consists of a broad band or as it might otherwise be conceived, a double row of large triangular features with a white zigzag line passing through its middle. The name here is the same as for an ordinary zigzag of colored material. In fig. 141 a

variant of this design is shown. This design is in all respects the same as that in fig. 140, except that occupying the center of the white zigzag space is a line in color. This becomes more of a complex pattern and is, according to the universal Pomo custom, given names indicative of this complexity. By the Northern Pomo it is called datō'ī kata dilē tsīyōtsīyōka, *design empty in-the-middle zigzag*. By the Central Pomo shorter descriptive names are given: tsīyō'tsīyō tcī lala, *zigzag design in-the-middle*, or tsīyō'tsīyō le'Lan, *zigzag in-the-center*. Eastern informants gave this pattern the names kaca'icai kalūītūduk dzīyōdzīyō, *butterfly striped-watersnake zigzag*, and xaga' dilē gaiya kalū'tūruk dzīyōdzīyō, *arrowhead in-the-middle gaiya striped-watersnake zigzag*.

Another form of horizontal zigzag, virtually the same as that in fig. 139 except that it is comparatively very broad, is shown in fig. 142. Its names are the same as for the zigzag of fig. 139.

The zigzag represented in fig. 143 differs from the last only in that its angles are very acute. It is, however, specially named by most informants. The Northern Pomo call it tsīyō'tsīyōka katca'k *zigzag arrowheads*, mina-datē'kama katcak, *crossing arrowhead*, and datī'pka, *sharp-points*. Central informants called it tsīyō'tsīyō katca-mset, *zigzag arrowheads-sharp*, and katca'-mset,

*arrowheads-sharp*. Eastern informants called it xaga' dzīyōdzīyō, *arrowhead zigzag*, and xaga'-dīset, *arrowhead-projecting*.
As before stated, the general term zigzag is applied to this as well
as to other similar designs.

Figs. 144 to 147 show zigzags consisting of narrow lines, every
alternating one of which is vertical instead of both lines of each
pair having the same slant as in the designs just described.   Of

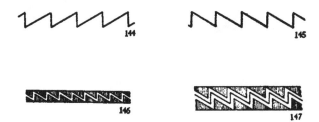

these designs the one shown in fig. 144 was called by informants
simply *zigzag*.   Those in figs. 145 and 146 were called not only
zigzag but by Northern and Central informants *grasshopper-
elbow*, cakō'-bīya, and cakō'-pīya, respectively.   In the case of
the design shown in fig. 146 some Northern informants gave the
name katca' dilē dzīyōdzīyō cīden, *arrowheads in-the-middle zigzag lead*, while certain Eastern informants also gave the names
xaga' dilē gaiya dzīyō'dzīyō gadīl, *arrowhead in-the-middle gaiya
zigzag passing-along*, and dzīyōdzīyō xō'nawa xaga, *zigzag on-
both-sides arrowheads*.   This design has been found in but a few
instances.

One case has been found of the design shown in fig. 147, to
which the name *zigzag* is applied by the people of all these Pomo
divisions.   Also among the Northern Pomo the name datōī datī'p-
ka dilē dzīyōdzīyō cīden, *design sharp-points in-the-middle zigzag lead* was found.

There are a number of rarely occurring zigzag designs consisting of comparatively wide lines varying greatly in length.   Some
are so short as to give the distinct impression of small rectangular or rhomboidal figures hitched together by their corners,
while others are so long as to give the impression of true linear
figures.   Various arrangements of designs of this kind are shown

in figs. 148 to 154.   Some, as that in fig. 154, have comparatively long narrow necks or connecting lines, while others, such as those in figs. 149 and 151 have none at all.   To all of these, the general term *zigzag* is applied by informants of all of the three dialectic divisions under consideration.   In the case of the design shown in fig. 153 the name bicĕ'-maō, *deer-back,* was also given by one Northern informant, though he at the same time stated that it

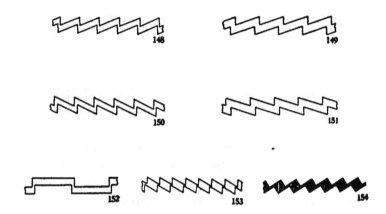

was a new kind of *deer-back* design and not the regular aboriginal pattern of that name.   Another name given was kase'tka, *sharp-points.*   One Central informant gave the name pdŭ'-cna, *acorn-head (or cup),* to this design.   The design represented in fig. 154 was called by two Northern informants cakō'-bīya, *grasshopper-elbow;* by a Central informant kapō'kpōkō kakaiûtcōm, *spotted kakaiûtcōm,* and by one Eastern informant bŭ'-dilē, *potato-fore-head.*   All these designs are comparatively rare, some having so far been found but once.

Fig. 155 shows a design found upon only one basket.   Northern Pomo informants spoke of this as dzī-yō'dzīyō dilē cīket, *zigzag in-the-middle stripe.*   Central informants called it tsīyō'-tsīyō sībo katcōm, *zigzag three together;* and some Eastern informants gave the names kalŭ'tūduk na tsawal-mīsak, *striped-watersnake and (or with) sunfish-rib,* and bŭ'-dilē dzīyōdzīyō, *potato-forehead zigzag.*

In the first of these Eastern names, the term striped-watersnake refers to the heavy vertical lines, and sunfish-rib to the lighter slanting ones.

156                              157

There are certain patterns which may be termed compound zigzags, that is, large zigzags which are composed of small zigzag lines. Designs of this sort are shown in figs. 156 to 162, to all of which the Indians gave the name *zigzag*, though to some of them other names were given as well. All these designs, except those in fig. 162, occur only as elements in complex pattern consisting of a horizontal band of large triangles, such as is shown in fig. 25, having the central space filled with one of these zigzag elements. Such complex patterns, containing the design elements shown in figs. 156 and 157, are called by the Northern Pomo datō'ī kata dilē tsīyō'tsīyō cīden, *design empty in-the-middle zigzag lead,* and by the Eastern Pomo xaga' dilē gaiya dzīyō'dzīyō gadil, *arrow-head in-the-middle gaiya zigzag passing along (plural).* No translation was obtained from Central informants for such a pattern as a whole, the component elements only being named. Neither one of these designs occurs very frequently.

About as frequently the pattern shown in fig. 158 is found. Owing to the fact that the zigzag portion is white it is necessary to show the entire pattern in order to give the zigzag itself. 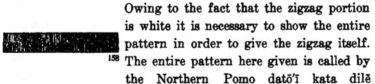 The entire pattern here given is called by the Northern Pomo datō'ī kata dilē tsīyō'tsīyōka, *design empty in-the-middle zigzag.* One informant also gave the name cakō'-bīya, *grasshopper-elbow,* on account of the sharp angles of the figure. Central informants called this pattern either simply *zigzag,* tsīyō'tsīyo, or *blank zigzag band,* kalū' tsīyōtsīyō ctot. Eastern informants called it *arrowheads in-the-middle gaiya zigzag,* xaga' dilē gaiya dzīyō'dzīyō. One informant also called it *zigzag-projecting,* dzīyō'dzīyō-dīset.

The design shown in fig. 159, while being an element in the center of a broad band of design (pl. 16, fig. 4) is itself some-

what complex.   Among the Central Pomo its name is kapŏ′kpōkō *ctot* lala sle′ma tcū-wan, *spotted band in-the-middle string stripe,* and among the Eastern Pomo bicĕ′-to xam tŭ′ntūn gadil, *deer stand-in among ants passing along (plural).*   The reason for the name ants appearing in this last case is that the white line in the middle of the pattern, as is shown in the illustration above referred to, appears more or less broken by colored fibers.   No name was obtained among the Northern Pomo for this particular portion of the pattern, but it as a whole was called datŏ′ĭ kata dilĕ katca′k daien, *design empty in-the-middle arrowhead collected.*

In figs. 160 and 161 a simple zigzag arrangement of rhomboidal figures, in one case white and in the other colored, is shown. Both these are called *spotted,* dapŏ′kpōkō, among the Northern and Central Pomo.   In addition, the design shown in fig. 161 is called by the Northern Pomo datŏ′ĭ kata dilĕ dasĕ-sĕ-tenka *design empty in-the-middle scattered along in a line,* and datŏ′ĭ dasetka, *design crossing.*   By the Central Pomo it is called dapŏ′-kpōkō lĕLan katca, *spots in-the-center arrowhead.*   By the Eastern Pomo it is called kaca′icai bū-dilĕ dzīyŏdzīyŏ, *butterfly potato-forehead zigzag,* xaga′ dilĕ gaiya xama paser gadil, *arrowhead in-the-middle gaiya mark tied-together passing along (plural),* and dzīyŏ′dzīyŏ xaga xo′′nawa dai, *zigzag arrowhead on-both-sides along.*   Both these figures occur quite frequently.

Two examples of the compound zigzag design shown in fig. 162 have been found.   This is called *zigzag* among all three Pomo divisions, but in addition it is called by the Northern Pomo dzīyŏ′dzīyŏ ūyŭl dana daie′nga, *zigzag upward placed-close-to-gether-in-a-row.*   By the Central Pomo it is also called tsīyŏ′tsīyŏ ūnaLiū, *zigzag crossing,* and by the Eastern Pomo kalel tsawa'l-mĭsak, *nothing sunfish-rib.*

One instance of the design represented in fig. 163 has been found. This was called by informants of all three divisions new or *white man's design.* It was also called *zigzag* by certain informants. One Eastern informant also spoke of it as *deer-back,* bicĕ'maō. ·

Another new or *white man's design* is shown in fig. 164. One Eastern informant, however, called this kaitsa'kai kama, *stretcher mark,* also the same informant said that it resembled the *deer-back* design, but was unlike either one.

A few cases of zigzag figures arranged vertically have been found. The names of such zigzags are in the main the same as those for zigzags arranged horizontally or diagonally. Certain informants, however, gave names other than zigzag and some used qualifying terms in connection with the terms signifying zigzag. The vertical narrow line zigzag (fig. 165) was called by

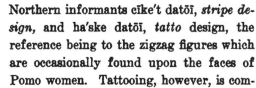

Northern informants cĭke't datōī, *stripe design,* and ha'ske datōī, *tatto* design, the reference being to the zigzag figures which are occasionally found upon the faces of Pomo women. Tattooing, however, is comparatively rare among the Pomo, and when used usually consists of from one to four straight vertical lines upon the chin and perhaps one or two small horizontal lines at the corners of the mouth. Zigzags are very rarely used by them in tattooing, although with the Yuki immediately to the North, among whom tattooing is more prevalent, they are quite common. Among Central informants this design was called *striped-watersnake,* msa'kale, as well as *zigzag,* and among Eastern informants it was called kalū'tūduk kaiyūlal dabel, *striped-watersnake upward stir (?).*

Two cases of a design practically identical with the last, except that the line which forms the zigzag is very wide, have been found.  This design is shown in fig. 166 and also in pl. 18, fig. 5.

It is called by informants of all three divisions *zigzag*.   Different informants of each division, however, use different forms of the term zigzag, some adding ka to the ordinary names for zigzag, as was mentioned when first speaking of zigzag designs.  Thus by the Northern and Central Pomo respectively it is called tsīyō'tsōyō and ka'tīyotīyō, and by the Eastern Pomo dzīyō'dzīyō and xa'tī'yōtī'yō.  In addition to these names, it is sometimes given more descriptive ones, as, among the Northern Pomo ū'yūl dana tsīyōtsīyō, *upward rub (?) zigzag;* among the Central Pomo tsīyō'tsīyō ūyūl kaa tcūwan, *zigzag upward daylight (?) stripe;* and among the Eastern Pomo kalū'tūduk tī'yōtī'yō, *striped-watersnake zigzag.*

The pattern shown in fig. 167 and consisting of a band of short broad zigzags was found upon one basket.  In general, the name given it is simply *zigzag* or *zigzag band,* though Northern Pomo informants also gave the more descriptive term tsīyōtsīyōka datsaibanem dilē dapī'dapīka, *zigzag broad-band in-the-middle small-figures.*  The idea of small-figures is not exactly clear in the schematic figure here shown, in which the narrow white lines appear as continuous.  As a matter of fact, this design occurs on a basket of plain-twined weave and the narrow white line is but one stitch, or more properly but one warp stick in width, thus making it more or less broken and giving the effect, not of a true narrow white line but of a zigzag row of fine white dots.  By Central informants it was called tsīyō'tsīyō ūyūl kana, *zigzag upward close.*  One Central informant also called it tsawa'l-msak, *sunfish-rib.*

Another one of these vertical zigzags is seen in fig. 168.  This design was called by Northern informants katca'k dase'tka datōī, *arrowhead crossing design,* and by Central informants kaa'i-kama kateltaimaū *ctot, crow-foot (or track) interlocking band,* and also simply kaa'i-kama *ctot, crow-foot (or track)* band.

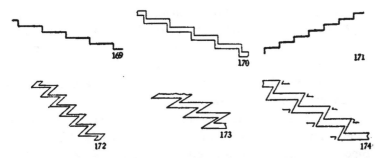

Of diagonal zigzags, there are a comparatively large number, some slanting very sharply toward the base line, others very gradually, some with their component lines making right angles with each other, others with their component lines making various acute angles with each other, some with longer or shorter connecting lines or necks of various widths, and some with no connecting necks at all. These various diagonal zigzags are shown in figs. 169 to 194. As before stated, there are two separate terms applied to zigzags in each of the three Pomo divisions under

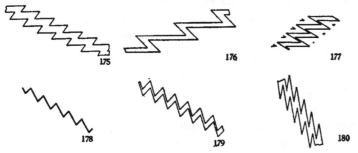

consideration, one being a compound of the other with the addition of ka or xa before it and certain phonetic changes within it. The difference, if there be any, between these terms does not seem clear to the Indians, so that within the same dialectic group, one may be used by one informant and the other by another in speaking of the same design. This is particularly noticeable in connection with the diagonal zigzags as shown in figs. 169 to 180, which have connecting lines or necks. In practically all cases each of these designs is called by both names by different informants speaking the same dialect. By the Northern and Central Pomo they are called tsīyō′tsīyo, ka′tīyōtīyō and katī′yō′tī′yō, while by the Eastern Pomo the names dzīyō′dzīyo, xatīyō′tīyō, katīyō′tiyō and katī′yo′tī′yō are used. The last four of these terms are practically the same but the variations are very distinctly noticeable. By some Northern and Central informants they are also called tsīyō′tsīyōka and by some Eastern informants they are called dzīyō′dzīyōka.

It is not feasible to illustrate with exactness each distinct form of zigzag found, since practically no two are exactly alike in their proportions, etc. Those here given are therefore types of their respective classes and in such designs as are shown in figs. 169 and 170 considerable differences in the length of the horizontal lines and of the connecting lines or necks are found. As these approach more nearly the form of rectangles with their corners joined, such as those in fig. 95, they are sometimes differently named by certain informants. For instance, some Northern and Central informants named certain patterns, of which figs. 169 and 170 are the typical forms, *deer-back*, bicē′-maō and pcē′meō, respectively, while Eastern informants named these same figures *potato-forehead* and *ants mark*, bū′-dilē and tū′ntun kama, respectively. The same is true of the design shown in fig. 172. Similarly, one Central informant called the sharp angled zigzag in fig. 179 *deer-elbow*, pcē′-pīya and one Eastern informant called the design shown in fig. 178 *grasshopper-elbow*, cakō′-bīya. The very sharp angled zigzag represented in fig. 180 was also called by Northern informants katca ū′yūl dana daienga, *arrowhead upward rub (?) placed-close-together-in-a-row*, by Central informants katca′-mset dītcī, *arrowhead-sharp design*, and by Eastern informants xaga′-daset dzīyōdzīyō, *arrowhead-barbed zigzag*.

The diagonal zigzag designs just mentioned are found in use by themselves as entire patterns, but they are found perhaps more frequently in combination with other design elements to make complex patterns. The most commonly occurring of these diagonal zigzag designs are the ones shown in figs. 174, 169, 172 and 180, named in the order of their frequency.

In figs. 181 to 186 are shown a series of rhomboidal figures of different proportions arranged in diagonal lines, forming zigzags. In all these, each one of the small rhomboidal figures is so placed that two of its diagonally opposed corners touch similar corners of the adjacent rhomboidal figures. To each of these designs the general name *zigzag* is given but, in addition, certain other names are given to some of them. The design shown in fig. 181 has been called by Northern informants bicē'-maō, *deer-back,*

and in one case it was called katca'k, *arrowhead.* By Central informants the name katca'-mtil, *arrowhead-slender* was given, while by some Eastern informants the names bicē'-maō, *deer-back,* bicē-yaō, *deer-teeth,* bicē' tō, *deer stand-in,* and cō-bax kama, *east this mark,* were given. This design is very frequently found combined with large triangular design elements to form a complex pattern, similar to that shown in fig. 55. Such a pattern is shown also in pl. 17, fig. 5.

Similarly in the case of the design shown in fig. 182 Northern

informants sometimes called it datō'ī maa, *design acorn,* bicē'-maō, *deer-back,* and katcak, *arrowhead.* Central informants sometimes called it kapō'kpōkō, *spotted* and Eastern informants gave the name bicē'-tō kama, *deer stand in mark.* This design occurs quite frequently as an element compounded with large triangular figures to form a complex pattern. It is much less frequently met with, however, than the design shown in fig. 181.

A few instances of the design shown in fig. 183 have been

found. In all cases it is the middle design elements of a pattern of large triangles, such as is shown in fig. 55. Names other than zigzag were obtained for this, as follows: among the Northern Pomo datōī dati'pka, and dase'tka, *design sharp-points* and *crossed* respectively; among the Central Pomo katca'-mtil, *arrowhead-slender,* and cō-ma ke'kama, *east-place from mark;* and among the Eastern Pomo datīp, *sharp pointed,* also dzīyō'dzīyō-dīse't *zigzag-projecting.*

A very few examples of the design shown in fig. 184 have been found.  The only names other than *zigzag* obtained for this design were found among the Central Pomo.  One informant called it katca', *arrowhead,* and another kaa'i-kama, *crow-foot (or track).*

The designs shown in figs. 185 and 186 have thus far been found in but one case each.  The one name, other than *zigzag,* obtained for either of these was found among the Central Pomo, where one informant gave pcĕ'meŏ, *deer-back,* as another name for the design of 186.

The peculiar zigzag seen in fig. 187 was given names as follows: by the Northern Pomo dzīyŏ'dzīyo or tsīyŏ'tsīyŏ, *zigzag,* bŭ'-dilĕ, *potato-forehead,* which it derives from the slanting rows

of small rectangles, and tsakŏ'tsakōka, *zigzag.*  By the Central Pomo it is called tsīyŏ'tsīyŏ, *zigzag;* and by the Eastern Pomo bŭ'-dilĕ dzīyŏ'dzīyŏ, *potato-forehead zigzag.*  This unusual pattern was found upon but one basket.

Another peculiar pattern found upon a single basket is that shown in fig. 188.  This was called by informants of all three of the Pomo divisions zigzag, but by Northern and Eastern informants it was also called bicē'-maŏ, *deer-back,* and by Central informants kaa'i-kama, *crow-foot (or track).*

Occasionally a crossing zigzag is found.  Such a design is shown in fig. 189.  Designs of this kind were called by Northern informants tsīyŏ'tsīyŏka kana daye'tkamū, *zigzag close meet (plural);* by Central informants ka'tīyŏtīyŏ ūnaLiū, *zigzag crossing;* and by Eastern informants dzīyŏ'dzīyŏ wīnalīhempke, *zigzag crossing.*

The Z shaped designs represented in figs. 190 and 191 were found upon only a few baskets. The former, in fact, was found but once. It was called by Northern Pomo informants bicĕ'-maŏ datsa'ibanem *deer-back broad-band;* by Central informants kaa'i-kama, *crow-foot (or track);* and by Eastern informants Lal-a-pa,

190                                                191

*goose-excrement.* The design in fig. 191 was variously named by different informants. By the Northern Pomo it was called ka'tīyŏtīyŏ, *zigzag,* bicĕ'-maŏ datŏī, *deer-back design,* datī'pka datsaibanem, *sharp-points broad-band,* and ditce'kka, said to be the name given to a game in which a wooden or other skewer is thrust through a string of fish vertebrae as it passes through the air. Central informants gave this design the names ka'tīyŏtīyŏ ctot, *zigzag band,* and kaa'i-kama, *crow-foot (or track).* In one case also in which this design appears near the edge of a flat plate-form basket it was called baiya'kaŭ, *finishing design,* this being the name applied to almost any design near the border or opening of a basket. This, however, is one of the rare instances in which such a border or finishing design is not a row of small rectangular figures. Eastern informants gave the names of this design as dzīyŏ'dzīyŏ and katī'yŏ'tī'yŏ, both meaning *zigzag,* xama' dītīp, *mark sharp,* and cŏ bax kama, *east this mark.* One informant also called it xatī'yŏtī'yŏ xŏtoagan, *zigzag, running along-in-pairs.*

The zigzag design shown in fig. 192 was found in use as the central element of a complex diagonal pattern of large triangles, similar to the pattern shown in fig. 55. The entire pattern was called by Northern Pomo informants datŏ'ī kata dilē kaa'i-kama daienga, *design empty in-the-middle crow-foot (or track) placed-close-together-in-a-row.* By another Northern informant the name tsūhū'n, for which no translation was obtained, was given. Among the Northern, as well as among the Central Pomo this design element alone was called *crow-foot (or track)*. Among the Eastern Pomo it was given the name which has heretofore been roughly translated as *stretcher*. Two names for the pattern as a whole were obtained among informants of this division of the Pomo, xaitsa'kai xō''nawa kaga gadil, *stretcher on-both-sides arrowheads passing along,* and xaga' dilē gai xaitsa'k kama, *arrowheads in-the-middle gai stretcher mark.*

In figs. 193 and 194, both of which are of comparatively rare occurrence, are shown two other designs which are usually called by all informants *zigzag*. Some Northern informants have given certain examples of these designs the name *deer-back,* bicĕ'-maō as have also some Eastern informants. Central informants usually called them *zigzag,* though kaa'i-kama, *crow-foot (or track)* was also used.

### Diamond Shaped Elements.

Designs composed of diamond shaped figures with their long axes horizontal, such, for instance, as those in figs. 195, 196 and 197 are quite frequently met with, the last, however, being the least uncommon of the three. The design shown in fig. 195 is called by the Northern Pomo *turtle-back,* kawī'na-tcīdik, and by the Central and Eastern Pomo kawī'na-ūtca and xana'dīhwa-kōī, respectively, both terms signifying *turtle-neck*. One Eastern informant added lik, signifying *band,* to the name turtle-neck. Central informants also called this design *acorn-head (or cup),* pdū'-cna, though this name is more frequently applied to the designs seen in figs. 196 and 197. One Northern informant called this design datī'pka datōī, *sharp-points design,* and one Central informant, who evidently considered this a modern design, gave the name wada'ha tcī. Wada'ha was defined by this informant as the name given to the Spanish game of *cards* and the design was said by her to

have been taken from these cards. Most informants, however, claimed this as an aboriginal pattern.

The design shown in fig. 196, consisting of lines crossing in  such a fashion as to inclose white diamond shaped spaces, is named with regard to both the crossing lines and the inclosed blank areas. Here as elsewhere, the only means of making a diagonal line is by a series of small rectangular figures, which result in an irregular step shaped line. These crossing lines of small rectangles are called by the Northern Pomo bicē'-meō mina-datē'kama, *deer-back crossing.* By the Eastern Pomo these lines are called bicē'-maō wīnalī-hempke, *deer-back crosing,* or bū'-dilē wīnalīhempke, *potato-fore-head crossing.* They may be conceived of as zigzag lines instead of deer-back or potato-forehead designs, in which case their name is dzīyō'dzīyō wīnalīhempke, *zigzag crossing.* One informant of the Central dialect also called this design *zigzag crossing,* tsīyō'-tsīyō ūnaLiū. Most Central informants, however, gave the name *acorn-head (or cup)* pdū'-cna, referring more to the inclosed diamond shaped spaces than to the lines themselves. Some Central informants gave the compound name *deer-back acorn-head (or cup),* pcē'-meō pdū-cna. Northern informants also named the diamond shaped space kawī'na-tcīdik, *turtle-back,* and Eastern informants named it kana'dīhwa-kōī, *turtle-neck.* One Eastern informant gave the compound name kana'dīhwakōī bū-dilē wīnalīhempke, *turtle-neck potato-forehead crossing.*

In fig. 197 is shown a design which is practically the negative of 196. By Northern informants this pat-  tern was called datō'ī kata dilē kawi'na-tcīdik, *design empty in-the-middle turtle-back.* Datō'ī kata refers to the triangular figures along the sides of the pattern and kawī'na-tcīdik to the diamond shaped figures included between these lines of triangles. These diamond shaped figures were also called by another Northern informant dapō'kka, *large-spots.* Central informants called this pattern simply pdū'-cna and pdū-cna ctot, *acorn-head (or cup)* and *acorn-head (or cup) band,* thus making no particular mention of the triangular figures of the

pattern.   Eastern informants gave the names kaca′icai wīnalīhempke, *butterfly crossing,* which refers to the large triangular
figures, and dzīyō′dzīyō xŏldabĕhmak, *zigzag meet,* referring to
the crossing white lines.   The name bū-dilĕ-ūī, *potato-forehead
eye,* was also given by some informants as the name for this pattern.

The diamond shaped pattern shown in fig. 198 has been found
in but a few instances.   It is generally considered by informants practically the same

as those in figs. 196 and 197.   Certain
Northern informants gave the name da-
tī′pka xŏltū dzīyō′dzīyo cīten, *sharp points
on-both-sides zigzag straight-band,* the important part of the design according to the Indians being the lines bordering the diamond shaped figures.   Central informants noted these bordering
lines in a different way, calling them kamtitalī-ū′ī-kūwī, *killdeer-
eye-brow,* a name said to be derived from the dark line over the
eye of that bird.

In figs. 199 and 200 are shown diamond shaped designs which
are of very rare occurrence.   Both were called new or white
man's designs by certain informants of all three dialects, but by
other informants Indian names were given, though all seemed
to consider them not aboriginal designs.   Northern dialect informants called the design of fig. 199 dapō′kka, *large spots,*
datī′pka, *sharp points,* and datōī sīsī′sīsi, *design small-figures.* Informants of the Central division gave the names katca′-mtip,
*arrowhead-slender,* katca ō′pit-ai, *arrowhead sharp pointed (plural)* katca kapōkpōkō, *arrowhead spotted.*   In cases where these
figures occur singly or in what has been termed individual arrangement, they were called kapō′kpōkō tatū *spotted single (or
one).*   Eastern informants also connected this design with the
arrowhead, calling it xaga′-mīset, *arrowhead-sharp.*   Northern
informants called the design shown in fig. 200 datōī tcadō′lai,

*design globular (plural)*. Some Central informants gave the name katca kapō'kpokō, *arrowhead spotted*, while Eastern informants gave the name kama dītas, *mark dot*.

Diamond shaped figures arranged with connecting lines such as are shown in fig. 201 were called by the Northern Pomo *grass-*

*hopper-elbow*, cakō'-bīya, as well as dīse't-ka, *crossed*, datōī bīyō'bīyō, *design little pieces*, and datīpka, *sharp points*. Central and Eastern informants usually gave simply *zigzag* as the name of this design. One Central informant, however, gave the name katca' lala tsīyō'tsīyō kaden, *arrowhead in-the-middle zigzag follow-up*, while one Eastern informant gave xaga' dilē dai dzīyō'dzīyō gadil, *arrowhead in-the-middle along zigzag passing-along*. This design has been found upon only a few baskets.

The design of squares in fig. 202 was called by the Northern Pomo *turtle-back*, kawī'na-tcīdik; by the Central Pomo turtle-neck, kawīna-ūtca, and *acorn-head (or cup)*, pdū'-cna; and by the Eastern Pomo *turtle-neck*, kana'dīhwa-kōī. One Eastern informant also gave the name xaga' gaūcaiyaūhmak, *arrowheads interlocking (or sticking-through-between-one-another)*. Only two examples have thus far been found of this design.

One example of the design of hollow squares shown in fig. 203 has been found. This was called by Central Pomo informants pdū'-cna, ctot, *acorn-head (or cup) band*, and by Eastern informants bū'-dilē-ūī, *potato-forehead-eye*.

A couple of instances of a design like that in fig. 204 have been found on baskets of the diagonal-twined weave. They appear as white line figures within a large triangle as is shown in pl. 16, fig. 2. By Northern informants this design was called dapō'dapōka, *spotted*, or simply daū, the name usually applied to the break in a horizontal band of design. Central informants called it pdū'-cna, *acorn-head (or cup)*, and tsīyō'tsīyō, *zigzag*.

Eastern informants gave the name dzīyŏ′dzīyŏ wīnalīhempke, *zigzag crossing*.

In figs. 205 to 209 are shown five designs which are by Northern informants usually called *turtle-back*, kawī′na-tcīdik, and by Central and Eastern informants *turtle-neck*, kawī′na-ūtca, and kana′dīhwa-kōī respectively. The design of fig. 205 is called by the Central Pomo pdū′-cna, *acorn-head (or cup)* and on account

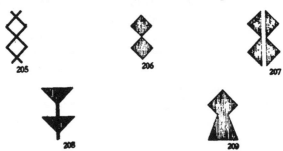

of the crossing lines which are of necessity composed of small rectangular figures, the name pcĕ′-meŏ, *deer-back* is also given, sometimes the two being combined into pcĕ′-meŏ pdū-cna, *deer-back acorn-head (or cup)*; and Central informants also gave pcĕ′-meŏ ŭnaliŭ, *deer-back crossing*. By Eastern informants bū′-dilĕ wīnalīhempke, *potato-forehead crossing*, was given as one name for this design. One Eastern informant gave as the name of the design of fig. 207 kana′dīhwa-kōī dilĕ dūta′p gīwal, *turtle-neck in-the-middle wide-mark running-along*. All the designs called turtle-neck by Eastern and Central Pomo informants are usually called turtle-back by those of the Northern dialect. One informant, however, gave the name kawī′na-kū′, turtle-neck, to the design shown in fig. 209. Similarly, an Eastern informant called the design of fig. 205 xana′dīhwa-*kidī*, *turtle-back*.

The rectangular design with points shown in fig. 210 has been

called *turtle-foot*, kawīna-kama, and kana′dīhwa kama. It was claimed by most informants to be a new or *white man's design*. Some informants claim that there is no design called turtle-foot, while one Northern informant described a turtle-foot design, consisting of a more or less circular figure with four or five projecting points about it.

*Quail Plume Elements.*

The designs shown in figs. 211 to 222 show various simple and complex forms of the *quail-plume design.* These various designs take their names from the club-shaped plume of the California valley quail, *Lophortyx californicus.* The quail plume is called by the Northern and Central Pomo caka'ka kēya, and by the Eastern Pomo cag'ā'x-xe or caka'ga-ke. This is, on the whole, the most common of the animal designs used by the Pomo and is the only one to which the Pomo attach any realistic significance. The element itself always bears the name quail-plume, but the names of the complex patterns vary greatly according to the many and varied other elements with which it is combined. In fig. 211 is shown the most simple form of the quail-plume design,

in which the plain quail-plume figures appear uncombined with any other design 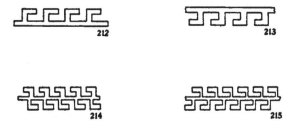 elements. In this particular and most

211

typical case the vertical line or stem of the quail plume is narrower than the horizontal line. In some cases, however, the two lines are of the same width. In figs. 212 to 215 are shown four patterns composed of quail plumes combined with straight lines. These were called by the Northern Pomo simply *quail-plume broad-band,* caka'ga-kēya datsa'ibanem. By the Central and Eastern Pomo, however,

212

213

214

215

more descriptive names were given, as follows: *striped-watersnake band side quail-plumes,* msa'kale ctot tūl caka'ga-kēya, by the Central Pomo, and *striped-watersnake and (or with) quail-plumes,* xalū'tūduk na cag'ā'x-xe, *striped-watersnake in-the-middle gaiya quail-plumes,* xalū'tūduk dilē gaiya caga'ga-xe, *quail-*

plumes *in-the-middle gaiya striped-watersnake*, caga'ga-xe dilē gaiya kalū'tūduk, and *striped-watersnake quail-plumes on-both-sides passing-along*, kalū'tūduk cakaga-xe kō'nawa gadil, by the Eastern Pomo. Of these four designs, the one shown in fig. 214 is the most common, though none of them occur very frequently.

The design shown in fig. 216, which as been found but once, was called simply quail-plumes. One informant stated that the rectangular figure, in the middle was started for an arrowhead but was never finished.

216

217

In fig. 217 is shown a design consisting of a large triangle or arrowhead, the sides of which are bordered by quail-plumes. This design which occurs quite frequently was called by Northern informants datō'ī kata xōl*tū* cakaga-kēya daien'na, *design empty on-both-sides quail-plumes placed-close-together-in-a-row,* and by the Central Pomo katca'-dalaū caka'ga kēya kōwaldakaden, *arrowhead-half quail-plumes following-on-the-outside,* katca'-dalaū caka'ga-kēya, *arrowhead-half quail-plumes* or caka'ga-kēya katca, *quail-plumes arrowhead.* In cases where the triangle is very sharp-pointed, the name given was katca'-mset tōl caka'ga-kēya, *arrowhead-sharp on quail-plumes.* The following names were obtained for this design from Eastern informants: xaga' xō'nawa caka'ga-xe gadil, *arrowhead on-both-sides quail-plumes passing along,* xaga' dile gaiya caga'ga-xe xama, *arrowhead in-the-middle gaiya quail-plume mark,* and xaga'na caga'ga-xe, *arrowhead and (or with) quail-plumes.* A band or circle of these arrowheads with quail plumes such as is shown in fig. 30, is occasionally found, particularly on large woven baskets. The name given to such a banded pattern is usually the same as the name of the single triangle with quail plumes, except that sometimes by the Eastern Pomo the name *butterfly* instead of arrowhead is given to the large triangles.

Diagonal rows of large triangles with quail plumes upon the upper side of the row, as shown in fig. 218, are occasionally found.

These are called by the Northern Pomo datō'ī kata tū caka'ga-kēya daienga, *design empty side quail-plumes placed-close-to-gether-in-a-row,* and by the Central Pomo caka'ga-kēya katca, *quail-plumes arrowheads.* By the Eastern Pomo they are called xaga' dilē gaiya caga'ga-xe xama, *arrowheads in-the-middle gaiya quail-plumes mark.*

218        219

Now and then crossing lines with quail plumes on their sides, as shown in fig. 219, are found. These designs were called by Northern informants datō'ī datapan tū caka'ga-kēya daienga, *design large area side quail-plumes placed-close-together-in-a-row* and caka'ga-kēya mīna-datē'kama, *quail-plumes crossing.* Central and Eastern informants also gave the name *quail-plumes crossing,* in the first case caka'ga-kēya ūnaLiū, and in the second caka'ga-xe wīnalīhempke.

Fig. 220 shows one of the more unusual quail-plume designs.

220

This was called by the Northern Pomo tsīyō'tsīyōka tū caka'ga-kēya daienga, *zigzag side quail-plumes placed-close-together-in-a-row.* By another informant it was called kale datsū'ttcīka, *white compressed,* and ditce'kka, the name of a game in which a slender wooden or bone skewer is thrust through a string of fish vertebrae as it moves through the air. By Central informants this design was called, in addition to *quail-plume,* katca'k-kasūltak, *arrowhead-long,* and katca'k katūk, *arrowhead elbow (?).* Informants of the Eastern dialect gave the names caga'ga-xe, *quail-plume,* caga'ga-xe gabil, *quail-plume long,* and xalū'tūduk kama, *striped-watersnake mark.*

In figs. 221 and 222 are shown designs commonly called *quail-plume* which also occur rarely. In addition to quail-plume, the design shown in fig. 221 was called by one Northern informant bita'mta, *mosquito,* and by another dikō'tka, which is another name for zigzag, meaning in the strictest sense *wavy.* By one

Central informant this design was called kaa'i-kama, *crow-foot (or track)*, and by another ctot mka'litcai, *band scattered (plural)*. One Eastern informant called this design caga'ga-xe batīl

mahwak xama, *quail-plumes batīlmahwak mark*. Some informants claimed both these designs to be modern or *white man's designs*.

### Miscellaneous Elements.

The design, resembling a zigzag, shown in fig. 223 was called by some Northern informants and by all Central informants kaa'i-kama, *crow-foot (or track)*. By Eastern informants the names given were dziyŏ'dzīyŏ, *zigzag*, and xaitsa'k xama, *stretcher mark*. This design, like the one in fig. 192, has thus far been found upon but one basket and, also like that figure, occurs as the middle element in a diagonal pattern of large triangles. The pattern as a whole is called by the Eastern Pomo xaga' dilē gaiya dzīyŏ'dzīyŏ gadil, *arrowheads in-the-middle gaiya zigzag passing along*, and dzīyŏ-dzīyŏ xŏtcagan xŏ'nawa xaga, *zigzag running-along-in-pairs on-both-sides arrowheads*. It was called by Northern informants datŏ'ī kata dilē datōī maa daien, *design empty in-the-middle design acorn collect*.

In figs. 224 and 225 are shown forms of a design commonly called *sunfish-rib*, tsawa'l-msak by the Central Pomo. Northern informants called the design of fig. 224 datŏ'ī bīyŏbīyŏ, *design little-pieces*, though most informants of all three divisions considered it a new or *white man's design*. These designs have been found in but one instance each.

In fig. 226 is shown a wing-like design called by some of the Northern Pomo kata'talak-ca datōī, *bat's-arm (or wing) design.* This design has so far been found in only one case and was claimed by Central informants to be a new or *white man's design,* while Eastern informants gave it the name *arrowhead* or *arrowhead-half,* xaga' or xaga'-daLaū.

Fig. 227 shows a design which has also been found in but one instance. By one Northern Pomo informant this design was called katcak dase'tka, *arrowhead crossing,* and by another katca'-mīset, arrowhead-sharp. One Northern informant gave the name *bear-foot (or track),* bita'-kama, to each one of the five large divisions or lobes of the figure. Eastern informants gave the names xaga' daset *arrowhead barbed,* and bī'ya kama, *elbow mark.*

There are occasional instances of star shaped designs with from four to several points. Such a design, a six pointed star, is shown in fig. 228. The largest number of points yet found is ten. Designs of this kind were usually called zigzag by informants of all three divisions. One Northern informant spoke of them as *zigzag circle,* tsīyō'tsīyōka tcadamūl. Central informants gave also the names *star* and *starfish,* kaa'mūl and steik, and one Eastern informant gave the name star, ūyahō'.

The designs shown in figs. 229, 230 and 231 were, in most cases, called new or *white man's designs.* Indian names, however, were given by several informants for these. One Northern informant called the design in fig. 229 datō'ī dītaska, *design spotted.* One Central informant called it kawī'na-ūtca, *turtle-neck,* and the names kalū' kama, *blank mark,* kaca'icai, *butterfly,*

and yanī'ya kama, *calico (a term derived from the Spanish) mark* were also obtained.   One Northern informant gave kī'-tana datōī *crab-hand (or claw) design,* as the name for the design shown in fig. 230.   The design shown in fig. 231 was called by some Northern informants datī'pka datōī, *sharp-points design,* and katca, *arrowhead,* by some Central informants.   One Eastern informant called this design, kama' dagol, *mark foolish (or nonsensical).*

There are various other new or white man's designs, such, for instance, as those shown on the upper four figures of pl. 29, which presents four different sides of the same basket. Here, although there are many separate designs, there are no two alike. Such designs are almost never given aboriginal names, but are simply called new, new style, or *white man's designs.* Other examples of these white man's designs are shown in figs. 5 and 6 of the same plate.   The terms signifying new among the Central and Eastern Pomo are cūwĕ' and ciwĕ' respectively.   White man is called in all three of the Pomo dialects here treated masa'n. Base't is the term in the Central dialect meaning bad or ugly and is often applied to an ill-shaped figure which resembles some aboriginal design.   Among these new fashioned or white man's designs, the human figure such as is shown in pl. 18, fig. 4, is noteworthy, as the Pomo formerly never used the human figure as a decoration for their baskets.   In addition to being called new or white man's design, this figure is also sometimes called tca by the Northern, tcatc by the Central, and gaūk by the Eastern Pomo, all three terms signifying man.

## PATTERNS.

As before stated, in considering Pomo basket designs and their names, a sharp distinction must be made between the design element, the simple elemental figure, and the pattern as a whole, the more complex figure composed of one repeated or two or more combined elements.   In discussing the designs shown in figs. 1 to 231 design elements have been mainly treated, the various forms of the same element being, as far as possible, shown in these figures.   The names of such design elements are very simple terms referring to animate objects, plants, natural or artificial objects, and geometric figures. The terms applied to complex patterns are compounded from these simple names of elements and are not in the nature of true simple names but are more of descriptive phrases which mention all the important elements constituting the complex pattern and give, in the main, the relation in which each stands to the other.

Such complex patterns may be composed of a single element repeated over and over again, as, for instance, superimposed rows of triangles, such as are shown in figs. 22, 23, 24, and 45, superimposed rectangles such as are shown in figs. 75, 81, and 82, or numerous parallel rows of rectangles such as those shown in fig. 95. Such a pattern is usually called by the name of the single element of which it is composed and these names have been treated in speaking of the design elements and their names. It should, however, be noted that these names of elements do not often occur unaccompanied by modifying terms, but usually have associated with them such qualifying and descriptive terms as crossing, double, and so on, descriptive of obvious peculiarities of form, size, number or arrangement of the elemental designs or of the larger figures formed by the combinations of elemental designs. An example of this is shown in fig. 97, which may be called either deer-back or potato-forehead crossing, or deer-back or potato-forehead acorn-cup, the last name arising from the diamond-shaped figure formed by the crossing lines of rectangles.

There are many complex patterns which are composed not of a single repeated element but of two or more different elements combined into a complex whole. Patterns of this sort are given complex names in which the chief, at least, of the design elements are mentioned, and the relations in which the constituent elements stand to one another are given, thus making the term by which such a pattern is designated a descriptive phrase, rather than a simple name. Informants differ somewhat in naming such patterns, some giving names much more fully descriptive than others; but none of them stop with a simple name such as is applied to a design element. The most skillful basket makers almost invariably give long descriptive phrase-names to their patterns, while those who seem less conversant with basketry and basket-making neglect to mention in their names the finer distinctive features of the pattern. The complex descriptive names must therefore be considered the typical and proper names for such patterns.

Of these more complex patterns those consisting of large triangular figures combined with various other elements are the most common. These may occur either in a diagonal or a horizontal arrangement, each of these methods being found in about equal numbers.

DIAGONAL OR SPIRAL PATTERNS.

### *Triangles with Zigzags.*

Among the diagonal patterns the double row of large isosceles triangles with some form of zigzag through its middle is one of the most common. Such patterns are shown in pl. 18, fig. 2, pl. 19, fig. 2, and pl. 22, fig. 1. Practically all diagonal patterns are arranged so that if followed from the bottom of the basket upward, they progress toward the left. The diagonal rows of triangles which form the chief elements are therefore those shown in figs. 18 and 20. Between these may appear almost any of the various forms of zigzag shown in figures 169 to 175, and 178 to 180. Any such combination of these elements is usually called by the Northern Pomo datŏ'ī kata dilē tsīyŏ'tsīyŏ cīden, *design empty in-the-middle zigzag lead.* Some Northern informants gave the same name but omitted the last term. One informant gave the name tsīyŏtsīyŏ data'pka, *zigzag large-area* upon one occasion, and others gave datōī kata dilē cakŏ'-bīya datōī, *design empty in-the-middle grasshopper-elbow design,* and datōī kata dilē kaa'i-kama daien, *design empty in-the-middle crow-foot (or track) collected,* in cases where the particular kind of zigzag used to fill the middle of the pattern resembled the elemental designs called grasshopper-elbow or crow-foot (or track) respectively. Central Pomo informants gave these patterns the names katca lala ka'tīyŏtīyo tcūwan, *arrowheads in-the-middle zigzag stripe,* katīyŏtīyŏ mtca'kōlai lēLan, *zigzag mtcakolai in-the-center,* ka'-tīyŏtīyŏ katca, *zigzag arrowhead,* and katīyŏtīyo lēLan, *zigzag in-the-center.* Eastern Pomo informants gave xaga' dilē gaiya

dzīyōdzīyō, *arrowheads in-the-middle, gaiya zigzag,* xaga-daLau
xam dzīyō'dzīyō cūdil, *arrowhead-half among zigzag lead,* and
dzīyō-dzīyō xo''nawa xaga, *zigzag on-both-sides arrowheads.* In
cases where the zigzag approaches nearly the form of the diagonal
line of rectangular figures called deer-back, the pattern may be
called xaga xam bicĕ'-maō, *arrowheads among deer-back,* or xaga
dilē bicĕ'-maō, *arrowheads in-the-middle deer-back.* Similarly,
if the zigzag is composed of figures resembling those called by the
Eastern Pomo goose-excrement, the pattern may be called xaga
dilē gaiya Lal-a-pa kama, *arrowheads in-the-middle gaiya goose-
excrement mark.*

Of the combinations of triangles with zigzags above mentioned
the one shown in pl. 22, fig. 1 is probably the most common, while
that shown in pl. 18, fig. 2 is rarely met with. In this, there is
really a third element, the small sharp points which project in-
wards from the sides of the large triangles. These, however, were
not mentioned by any of the informants, the names given for this
pattern being the same as for a similar pattern without these
sharp points. Diagonal patterns composed of large triangles and
zigzags such as those just mentioned are usually found in baskets
of the twined weaves, though coiled baskets such as those shown
in pl. 18, fig. 2, and pl. 19, fig. 2 are occasionally found with
these patterns. Usually, these patterns have a single zigzag in
the center, though a few cases, such as the one shown in pl. 19,
fig. 2, have been noted where double zigzags are used.

### Triangles with Rectangles.

Another diagonal pattern which is frequently found is the
double row of triangles with one or more rows of rectangular
figures, often squares, through its middle. Examples of such
patterns are shown in pl. 18, figs. 3, 5, 6, and pl. 19, fig. 1. These
patterns are called by the Northern Pomo datō'ī kata dilē bitūmtū
daienga, *design empty in-the-middle ants placed-close-together-
in-a-row,* datō'ī kata dilē datcēdatcenka, *design empty in-the-
middle datcedatcenka,* datō'ī kata dilē cīkīkītinka, *design empty
in-the-middle extending,* and dapī'dapīka katcak nētak, *small-
figures arrowheads throw.* Central Pomo informants gave these

patterns the names pcĕ-meŏ lēLan katca, *deer-back in-the-center arrowheads*, katca pcĕ-meŏ lala tcūwan, *arrowheads deer-back in-the-middle stripe*, katca dalaŭ pcĕ-meŏ malada tcūwan, *arrow-head-half deer-back near stripe*, and pcĕ-meŏ katca, *deer-back arrowhead*. Eastern informants called them xaga' xam tūntūn gīwal, *arrowheads among ants running-along*, xaga' xam tūntūn dabel, *arrowheads among ants stir* (?), this name being applied to a pattern in which the center is filled with a double row of small rectangles. Other names are xaga' dilē gaiya dzīyŏdzīyŏ kama, *arrowheads in-the-middle gaiya zigzag mark*, xaga' dilē gaiya tūntūn gadīl, *arrowheads in the-middle gaiya ants passing-along*, and bū'-dilē xŏ'nawa xaga, *potato-forehead on-both-sides arrowheads*. When the pattern consists of such elements as those above mentioned but arranged in crossing lines as shown in pl. 19, fig. 3, the name crossing is added to the above mentioned names, or shorter names mentioning the crossing of the lines of the pattern are used, as, for instance, pcĕ'-meŏ katca ūnaLiŭ, *deer-back arrowhead crossing* among the Central Pomo, and bū-dilē wīna'līhempke kama, *potato-forehead crossing mark*, among the Eastern Pomo. In any of these patterns, the space between the rows of large triangles may be filled either by a single or by a double row of rectangles, usually worked out in the colored fiber material as shown in pl. 18, figs. 5, 6, though sometimes in white as in pl. 19, fig. 1. These patterns occur quite frequently and are usually found on coiled baskets, being the only combination of diagonal rows of large triangles and other figures which are met with at all frequently upon coiled ware.

It occasionally happens that there are more than two rows of small rectangular figures occupying the central space between the double row of diagonally arranged triangles. There are instances where two or more rows of such a design element occupy the center of a double row of triangles which itself occupies the center of a double row of still larger triangles. Such a pattern is found in pl. 17, fig. 6, where crossing lines of this elaborate pattern are shown. Among the Northern Pomo such a pattern is called in full datŏ'ī kata dilē katcak dilē kale dapī'dapī diaenga datŏī mina-datēkama, *design empty in-the-middle arrowheads in-the-middle white small-figures placed-close-together-in-a-row de-*

*sign crossing.* By others it was given the shorter name bitū′mtū mina-datēkama, *ants crossing.* Central Pomo informants gave still simpler names for the pattern, as a whole, as, katca kapō′k-pōkō ūnaLiū, *arrowheads spotted crossing.* At the same time, however, they named the constituent elements separately. The large triangles on the lower sides of the crossing lines of the pattern are called tca′l-katca, *inward-arrowhead,* and those on the upper sides of the lines are called ko′l-katca, *outward-arrowhead.* The inner combination of small triangles and little dots is called tū′ntūn katca ūnaLiū lala, *ants arrowheads crossing in-the-middle.* Eastern Pomo informants gave such names as xaga dilē′ gaiya gadil, *arrowheads in-the-middle gaiya arrowheads passing-along,* xaga dilē′ gaiya tūntūn gadil, *arrowheads in-the-middle gaiya ants passing-along,* wīna′līhempke kama xam tūntūn, *crossing mark among ants,* and kama′ paser wīnalīhempke, *mark tied-together crossing.* By one informant only was the design called zigzag. The name given in this case was simply dzīyō′dzīyō wīnalīhempke, *zigzag crossing.* As was stated when speaking of designs called ants (figs. 75 and 76), the name of such a design is dependent upon the size of the constituent rectangles. In the present case, these rectangles are very small indeed. In fact, they are here so small that they consist of but a single woof element each and are to be considered as mere dots of color on the white background. It is just such design elements, extremely small in comparison with the other constituent elements of the pattern, that are called ants. In these elaborate patterns where there is a double row of triangles within another double row of still larger triangles there is usually found but the one design element occupying the space of the central double row of triangles. In some cases, on the other hand, there is nothing at all placed here, the center being unoccupied except by a blank white line. Such a pattern is called by the Northern Pomo datō′ī kata dilē katca′k daienga dilē dakīkītinka, *design empty in-the-middle arrowheads placed-close-together-in-a-row in-the-middle scattered-along-in-a-line.* By Eastern Pomo informants it is called xalū′tūduk hna xaga-daset, *striped-watersnake and (or with) arrowheads-barbed,* dilē dagal kalū′tūduk tcadim, *in-the-middle dagal striped-watersnake tcadim,* and kalū′tūduk kama dilē, *striped-watersnake mark in-the-middle.*    Shorter names were given by Central Pomo informants, *viz.*, katca-mtĭp kama, *arrow-head-sharp-pointed mark,* and katca-mti'l ctot, *arrowhead-slender band.*

### Triangles with Rhomboids.

Among the more commonly occurring patterns on Pomo baskets are those composed of two parallel rows of large triangles with one or two rows of rhomboidal figures filling the space between them.    Examples of such patterns are shown in pl. 16, figs. 2, 3, 5, and in pl. 22, fig. 3.    Northern Pomo informants usually gave the names datŏ'ĭ kata dilē katca'k daien, *design empty in-the-middle arrowhead collected.*    Usually only triangular figures are called arrowheads, but in  this case the sharp pointed rhomboidal figures are sometimes so called by the Northern Pomo. Another name for this pattern is datŏ'ĭ kata dilē datŏ'ĭ maa cīden, *design empty in-the-middle design acorns lead;* also datŏ'ĭ da-tĭ'pka dilē katcak daien, *design sharp-points in-the-middle arrowheads collected.*    Central Pomo informants referred to these centrally placed rhomboidal figures by the name *spotted,* kapŏ'kpŏkŏ, and called the entire design katca lala kapŏ'kpŏkŏ tcūwan, *arrowheads in-the-middle spotted stripe,* kapŏ'kpŏkŏ katca lala tcūwan, *spotted arrowheads in-the-middle stripe,* katca kapŏ'kpŏkŏ, *arrowheads spotted,* and kapŏ'kpŏkŏ lēLan, *spotted in-the-center.*    In cases where these rhomboidal figures are so arranged that they very much resemble a zigzag, as in pl. 22, fig. 3, they are sometimes called by the Central Pomo ka'tĭyŏtĭyŏ lala tcūwan, *zigzag in-the-middle,* or ka'tĭyŏtĭyŏ lēLan, *zigzag in-the-center,* or the name may be shortened to simply tsĭyŏ'tsĭyŏ kama, *zigzag mark.* One Eastern Pomo informant gave the name kapŏ'kpŏkŏ lala slema tcūwan, *spotted in-the-middle string stripe,* as the name of the pattern of pl. 22, fig. 3, thus in this name taking into account the presence of the narrow white line called string, while omitting to mention the large triangles.    Eastern Pomo informants seem to have in most cases considered these diagonal lines of rhomboidal figures as zigzags and they usually gave these patterns such names as xaga' dilē gaiya xa'tĭ'yŏtĭ'yŏ gĭwal, *arrowheads in-the-middle gaiya zigzag running-along,* xaga' kama dzīyŏdzīyŏ, *arrowheads mark zigzag,* dzīyŏ'dzīyŏ xŏ'nawa xaga, *zigzag on-both-sides arrowheads,* and dzīyŏ'dzīyŏ-dīset, *zigzag-projecting.* Certain of these patterns, however, some informants did not consider as zigzags and gave such names as xaga' dilē gaiya bicĕ'-yaŏ, *arrowheads in-the-middle gaiya deer-teeth,* xaga' dilē gaiya bicĕ-maŏ, *arrowheads in-the-middle gaiya deer-back,* kaga' dilē gaiya bicĕ-to kama, *arrowheads in-the-middle gaiya deer-stand-in-mark,* dilē gaiya xaga gaūcaiyaū'hmak, *in-the-middle gaiya arrowheads interlocking,* and xaga' dilē gaiya La'l-a-pa kama, *arrowheads in-the-middle gaiya goose-excrement mark.* Patterns of this kind are confined almost entirely to twined basketry.

### Triangles with Triangles.

A diagonal pattern is occasionally found consisting of two rows of large triangles with the space between them filled simply with one or two rows of small triangles. Such a pattern is shown in pl. 18, fig. 1. Patterns of this kind were called by Northern Pomo informants datŏ'ī kata dilē katca'k yŏ-wil, *design empty in-the-middle arrowheads downward,* and datŏ'ī kata dilē maa cīden, *design empty in-the-middle acorns lead.* Central Pomo informants gave the names katca'-mtil katca leLan, *arrowheads-slender arrowheads in-the-center,* and ctū' katca katca-dalaū leLan, *coiled-basket arrowheads arrowhead-half in-the-center.* Eastern Pomo informants gave the name xaga'-daLaū dilē xacai-cai, *arrowheads-half in-the-middle butterfly.*

### Triangles with Lines.

Baskets are occasionally found with patterns consisting of rows of large trangles with the central spaces occupied by one or more narrow lines. Such a pattern is shown in pl. 22, fig. 2. Some Northern Pomo informants called this pattern datŏ'i kata dilē kale cīte, *design empty in-the-middle white straight-lines.* In this pattern, however, the inner surfaces of the large triangles are serrated, so that it gives the appearance of a set of small triangular figures placed upon the sides of the large ones, which accounts for the fact that some Northern informants gave the names datŏ'ī kata dilē katca'k daien, *design empty in-the-middle arrowheads collected,* and datŏ'ĭ kata *tŭ* katca'k daien, *design empty side arrowheads collected.* One Central Pomo informant gave the name katca' lala slema tcĭyau, *arrowheads in-the-middle string tciyau,* while another gave the name msa'kale kama, *striped-watersnake mark,* and still another katca'-dalaū, *arrowhead-half.* Eastern informants gave the names xalū'tŭduk xŏ'- nawa xaga kama, *striped-watersnake on-both-sides arrowheads mark,* xalū'tŭdŭk hna xaga-daset, *striped-watersnake and (or with) arrowheads-barbed,* and xaga-daLaū-daset, *arrowheads- half-barbed.*

### Miscellaneous Patterns.

An unusual pattern is shown in pl. 22, fig. 2, in which short zigzags fill the space between two rows of large triangular figures, the zigzags being so placed that they are transverse to the general direction of the diagonal pattern. Northern Pomo informants gave this pattern the names datŏ'ĭ kata dilē kaa'i-kama daienga, *design empty in-the-middle crow foot (or track) placed- close-together-in-a-row,* datŏ'ĭ kata dilē datŏĭ maa daien, *design empty in-the-middle design acorns collected,* and datŏĭ datĭ'pka dile tsakŏtsakŏka, *design sharp-points in-the-middle zigzag.* Central dialect informants all gave this pattern the name kaa'i-kama, *crow foot (or track),* stating that while they, in this particular case named the white zigzags, because they were the most conspicuous, the name applied equally also to the small colored zigzags separating them. Eastern informants gave the names xaga' dilē gaiya dzĭyŏ'dzĭyŏ gadil, *arrowheads -in-the-middle gaiya zigzags passing-along,* xaga' dilē cŏ bax gadil, *arrowheads -in-the- middle east this passing-along,* xaga dilē' gaiya Lal-a-pa kama, *arrowheads in-the-middle gaiya goose-excrement mark,* and dzĭ- yŏ'dzĭyŏ xŏtcagan xŏ'nawa xaga, *zigzags running-along-in-pairs on-both-sides arrowheads.*

### Crossing Patterns.

Lines of pattern so arranged that they cross each other are found now and then upon Pomo baskets. Two such patterns, shown in pl. 19, fig. 3, and pl. 17, fig. 6, have already been discussed. These are very elaborate, particularly the second, which is composed of three distinct types of elemental figures. While crossing patterns are usually elaborate like these, much more simple ones are sometimes found, such for instance as the one shown in pl. 28, fig. 1, in which double rows of triangular figures cross each other, the space between the triangles of each row being entirely blank. Northern Pomo informants called this pattern katca′k dilē dakīkītinka, *arrowheads in-the-middle scattered-along-in-a-line,* and katca′k mina-datēkama, *arrowheads crossing.* Central informants gave the names katca′-mtil ūnaLiū, *arrowheads-slender crossing.* Eastern informants gave the names kalū′tūduk hna xaga-daset wīnalīhempke, *striped-watersnake and (or with) arrowheads-barbed crossing,* and wīnalīhempke dzīyō-dzīyō, *crossing zigzag.* In the first of these two names, the triangles are considered as arrowheads and the central line as the striped watersnake design, both of which are the usual conceptions for these elements. In the second name, however, the informants take no account of the white line in the middle but consider the double row of triangles as a zigzag. Central Pomo informants usually called plain white lines, such as are shown in this pattern, string, but they for some reason took no account of the white line through the middle of this pattern.

### Bordering Triangles.

Upon many diagonal patterns composed of these large triangles combined with other design elements there are rows of still smaller triangles placed on the slanting outer margins of the large triangles and at a little distance from them, so that a narrow white line separates the large triangle from the row of small ones. Such rows of small edging or bordering triangles are shown in fig. 55, and pl. 22, fig. 1, and pl. 16, fig. 2. These are called by the Northern Pomo simply *arrowhead,* katca′k, or *arrowhead-sharp,* katca′-mīset. By the Central Pomo they are usually called *arrowhead-sharp,* katca-mset, or *arrowhead-slender,* katca′-mtil, and by the Eastern Pomo they are called *arrowhead-projecting,* xaga′-dīset, or *arrowhead-small,* xaga-xūt. These large triangles are also sometimes bordered with similar triangular figures which are joined directly to the large figures, thus making them a part of the large triangle itself. Two examples of such triangles, one a very acute angled figure, the other much less so, are shown in pl. 18, fig. 3, and pl. 17, fig. 2. Both these points are called by the Northern Pomo katca'k-kasetka, *arrowheads-sharp-points*, by the Central Pomo katca'-mset, *arrowheads-sharp*, and katca'-mtil, *arrowheads-slender*, and by the Eastern Pomo xaga'-datĭp, *arrowheads-sharp-points*. Such points, particularly the more acute angled ones, are found edging the insides of the double rows of large triangles. In such cases, some informants mentioned the sharp points themselves, while others mentioned the white zigzag, which is the result of the presence of these points in colored fibers. Some Northern informants gave the names datŏ'ĭ kata dilē dasĭ'dasĭka, *design empty in-the-middle scattered*, and datŏĭ kata dilē katcak daienga, *design empty in-the-middle arrowheads placed-close-together-in-a-row*. Central informants gave the name katca lala tsĭyŏ'tsĭyŏ tcŭwan, *arrowheads in-the-middle zigzag stripe*, and Eastern informants gave the names xaga dilē gaiya xaga-daset xama, *arrowheads in-the-middle gaiya arrowheads-barbed mark*, and xaga'-mĭset xaga xŏ'-nawa gadil, *arrowheads-sharp arrowheads on-both-sides passing-along*.

### HORIZONTAL OR BANDED PATTERNS.

Elaborate patterns arranged horizontally or in bands about the surface of a basket, as was mentioned in the general discussion of design arrangement, are met with very frequently, especially upon baskets of the several twined weaves. They are, however, found less frequently upon coiled baskets. Among the twined baskets also these horizontal or banded patterns are much more frequently found upon the large globose storage and cooking baskets and upon the plate-form baskets used for sifting and as general utensils, than they are upon burden baskets where the diagonal arrangement prevails. Occasionally, of course, a burden basket with a horizontally arranged pattern is found, as, for instance, pl. 22, fig. 6, which shows zigzag and rectangular elements of different kinds, each element being itself repeated again and again in the horizontal band about the basket, and none of them being combined with any other element into a complex pattern. There are many of these horizontal patterns which, like the ones just mentioned, are composed of but a single element or perhaps two simple elements. Such figures are seen in pl. 17, fig. 3, in which the band near the top is composed of elements called *quail-plumes* and the lowest band is composed of quail plume elements separated by a narrow line called *striped-watersnake*. There are, however, many of the more elaborate horizontal patterns, the majority of which are composed of a double row of large isosceles right triangles such as is shown in fig. 25 combined with various elements, such as rhombodial figures, triangles, rectangles, zigzags, and others. Three of the more simple patterns composed of isosceles right triangles, the spaces between which are filled with smaller triangles, are shown in figs. 26, 27, and 31, and the names applied to them have been given in treating the subject of triangular design elements. Another example of a banded or horizontal pattern formed upon the large isosceles right triangles as a base, is shown in fig. 30, in which these large triangles are edged or bordered with what is called the *quail-plume* design. The names applied to this pattern by various informants have also been given in the part of this paper treating of triangular elemental designs. This pattern is also found in the uppermost band about the basket shown in pl. 16, fig. 4.

### *Triangles with Rhomboids.*

One of the most commonly occurring of this class of horizontal or banded patterns is the one in which the spaces between the large triangles are filled with rows of rhomboidal figures. The baskets shown in pl. 17, figs. 1, 4, and pl. 16, figs. 1, 4, show typical examples of this pattern. Northern Pomo informants usually gave these patterns the name datō'ī kata dilē katca'k datsai-banem, *design empty in-the-middle arrowheads broad-band*, or datō'ī kata dilē katca'k daien, *design empty in-the-middle arrowheads collected*. In patterns in which the rhomboidal figures are white instead of colored, as is the case in pl. 17, fig. 4, they were called by some informants datō'ī kata dilē kale katcak daien, *design empty in-the-middle white arrowheads collected*. Here again it is worthy of note that the name arrowheads is applied to these rhomboidal figures instead of being restricted entirely to triangular figures as is usually the case. Central Pomo informants universally called these rhomboidal elements *spotted*, kapō′kpŏkō, and usually gave as the name for this pattern simply *spotted in-the-middle*, kapō′kpŏkō lēLan. Some called them *spotted band*, kapō′kpŏkō *ctot*. Like the Northern Pomo, they also distinguished between the patterns with ordinary colored rhomboidal figures and those with white rhomboids, calling the latter kalū′ kapŏkpŏkō *ctot-blank spotted band*. In the case of a pattern in which the rhomboids appear with a white line running through their middle as is shown in pl. 16, fig. 4, the Central Pomo gave the name kapō′kpŏkō *ctot* lala sle′ma tcūwan, *spotted band in-the-middle string stripe*. Eastern Pomo informants gave this pattern the names xaga dilē gaiya bicĕ-tō kama gadil, *arrowhead in-the-middle gaiya deer-stand-in mark passing-along*, bicĕ-tō xam tŭn-tūn gadil, *deer-stand-in among ants passing-along*. That these informants gave the term ants in connection with these names is due to the fact that the white line which runs through the middle of the row of rhomboids is but a single stitch or warp stick wide, and is, in consequence of its diagonal trend, not entirely continuous but appears as a slightly broken line. Other names given for these patterns were xaga′ dilē gaiya xama paser gadil, *arrow-heads in-the-middle gaiya mark tied-together passing-along*, and dzīyō′dzīyō xaga xō′nawa dai, *zigzag arrowheads on-both-sides along*.

### Triangles with Triangles.

Another class of horizontal or banded patterns which occurs quite frequently is the class of patterns which are combinations of large isosceles right triangles with smaller triangles of various kinds. Examples of these are shown in figs. 26, 27, and 28, and in pl. 20. The small triangles which border the edges of the larger ones are usually of the isosceles right triangle type but may be set with their apexes in any one of the several possible directions. The names applied to such patterns by the Northern Pomo are datō′ī kata dilē katcak daienga, *design empty in-the-middle arrowheads placed-close-together-in-a-row*, and datō′ī kata xōltū datī′pka, *design empty on-both-sides sharp-points*. In one instance where fine broken lines similar to the ones shown in the

center of the rhomboidal figures in the band of design second
from the top in pl. 16, fig. 4, occurred between the inner double
row of small triangular figures, the name given it by Northern
Pomo informants was datō'ī kata dilē katcak dilē dapīdapīka,
*design empty in-the-middle arrowheads in-the-middle small-fig-*
*ures.* Central dialect informants called designs of this class
generally katca'-dalaū ctot, *arrowhead-half band,* or katca-dalaū
lē'Lan, *arrowhead-half in-the-center;* and in the case of the particular pattern shown in pl. 20, katca'-mset, *arrowhead-sharp,* and
katca-mtil, *arrowhead-slender.* Eastern Pomo informants gave
the names xaca'icai dilē gaiya xaga dzīyōdzīyō, *butterfly in-the-*
*middle gaiya arrowheads zigzag,* and xaca'icai wīnalīhempke kalū-
tūduk kōldaiyaūhmak, *butterfly crossing striped-watersnake meet-*
*together.* Some informants also gave such short names as xaca'i-
cai-dīset, *butterfly-projecting,* and dzīyō'dzīyō-dīset, *zigzag-pro-*
*jecting.*

### Triangles with Rectangles.

Banded designs consisting of a row of large isosceles right
triangles, the spaces between which are filled with rectangular
figures as is shown in the broad middle band of pl. 17, fig. 3, are
occasionally found. These zigzag rows of rectangular figures are
usually single, but double rows are occasionally found. The
rectangles themselves may be of various proportions and here
again the names applied to them vary according to the size of
the rectangles in question, as has been already explained in treating of the design elements shown in figs. 74 to 98. In the cases
of the particular designs concerning which informants have been
questioned, this variation of the naming of the rectangular elements by different informants is worthy of consideration. Some
of the Northern Pomo informants gave to patterns of this class
the names datō'ī kata dilē datcē'datcenka, *design empty in-the-*
*middle datcedatcenka,* and datō'ī kata dilē datōī maa cīden, *design*
*empty in-the-middle design acorns lead.* Another Northern informant called the rectangular elements of this pattern bitūmtū,
*ants,* and another called them bicē'maō, *deer-back.* All Central
informants gave the name pcē'-meō, *deer-back,* to these rectangular elements, usually giving as the name for the entire pattern

simply pcĕ'-meŏ, ctot, *deer-back band.*   Eastern informants gave
more descriptive names but with the same variation in the names
of the rectangular elements.   The names applied to these patterns by them were xaga' dilē gaiya *tŭn*tŭn gadil, *arrowheads
in-the-middle gaiya ants passing-along,* bū'-dilē dzīyŏdzīyŏ xŏ'-
nawa xaga, *potato-forehead zigzag on-both-sides arrowheads,* and
bicĕ-tŏ dilē gadil xaca'icai, *deer-stand-in in-the-middle passing-
along butterfly.*

## Triangles with Zigzags.

A few cases of a horizontal band of large triangles separated
from each other by white or colored zigzags such as those shown
in figs. 156, 157, and 158, and the upper broad band about the
basket shown in pl. 17, fig. 4, have been found, but these are on
the whole the most rarely occurring patterns of this general class.
Some informants gave simply the name *zigzag* to all such patterns but some of the Northern Pomo gave the name datŏ'ī kata
dilē tsīyŏtsīyŏ, *design empty in-the-middle zigzag,* and some Eastern informants gave a similar name xaga' dilē gaiya dzīyŏdzīyŏ,
*arrowheads in-the-middle gaiya zigzag.*   White zigzags included
between the double row of isosceles right triangles such as is
shown near the center of the basket in pl. 23, fig. 2, are very
common.   The name of such a design is in most cases the same
as that which is given above but some informants give *grasshopper-elbow* as the name for this sharp angled zigzag, as also
for such patterns as are shown in fig. 147.

### PATTERNS COVERING THE ENTIRE SURFACE.

In a large measure, elaborate patterns are confined to spiral
and horizontal or banded arrangements, but there are certain
cases in which the entire surface of a basket may be covered with
a pattern which may be considered neither truly spiral nor
banded in its arrangement but which at the same time, if looked
at from another point of view, is not only both spiral and banded
but crossing as well.   Such, for instance, are the patterns shown
in figs. 35 and 36, and also in pl. 22, fig. 4, and pl. 16, fig. 6.

There are no special names used by the Indians for this particular arrangement, the names given to patterns of this kind being the same as though they were arranged in any one of the ordinary manners. Similar to these is the arrangement such as is shown in pl. 16, fig. 3, which is generally considered by the Indians as banded.

As before stated, there are various combinations of design elements other than these elaborate patterns composed of isosceles right triangles and other elements, but typical examples of practically all of the remainder of these combinations are shown in the schematic figures given in the first part of this paper. To attempt to show every combination and variation in minute detail would be not only useless, since the names for similar though not identical combinations are the same, but it would be wholly impracticable as it would involve the illustration of a very great number of baskets. Though they may bear the same names and may be alike in all essential features, minor differences make it almost impossible to find two patterns which are in all respects identical. Nearly all of the more elaborate patterns have isosceles right triangles as the chief elements and typical examples of these have just been given, together with their descriptive names. The names of the less elaborate combinations, typical examples of all of which are shown in the schematic figures above referred to, are given in speaking of the various design elements.

## ELEMENTAL NAMES.

There are in all fifty-four names of Pomo design elements which may be classified as follows: animate objects or parts of animate objects, plant names, names of artificial or natural objects, names of more or less geometric figures, miscellaneous names, and names entirely of modern origin, or if of aboriginal origin applied only to designs introduced in modern times. The following table shows the total number of names of each of these classes found in each of the Pomo divisions considered, the total number of these names in common use in each of these three divisions, and finally the total numbers found in all three divisions and the total numbers in common use in all three divisions.

| | Total number | | | In common use | | | Total in all divisions | In common use in all divisions |
|---|---|---|---|---|---|---|---|---|
| | N | C | E | N | C | E | | |
| Animate objects ............ | 16 | 15 | 11 | 10 | 10 | 8 | 23 | 12 |
| Plants ............................... | 3 | 1 | 2 | 1 | 1 | 1 | 5 | 2 |
| Artificial and natural objects ........................ | 3 | 3 | 3 | 2 | 2 | 2 | 6 | 4 |
| Geometric figures ......... | 7 | 2 | 2 | 3 | 2 | 1 | 7 | 4 |
| Miscellaneous ................ | 4 | 5 | 4 | 4 | 2 | 2 | 7 | 4 |
| Modern ........................... | 2 | 6 | 3 | 1 | 2 | 2 | 6 | 2 |
| Totals ................ | 35 | 32 | 25 | 21 | 19 | 16 | 54 | 28 |
| Truly aboriginal names | 33 | 24 | 22 | 20 | 17 | 14 | 48 | 26 |

### NAMES OF DESIGN ELEMENTS.

| *Animate objects* | *Northern* | *Central* | *Eastern* |
|---|---|---|---|
| deer-back | bicĕ'-maδ | pcĕ'meδ | bicĕ'maδ |
| striped-watersnake | mīsa'kalak | msa'kale | kalŭ'tŭduk |
| | masa'kalak | | kalŭ'tŭruk |
| quail-plume | caka'ka kĕya | caka'ka kĕya | caka'ga-ke |
| | | | cag' a'x-xe |
| ant | bitŭ'mtŭ | tŭ'ntŭn | tŭ'ntŭn |
| butterfly | kaca'icai | kaca'icai | xaca'icai |
| deer-teeth | bicĕ'-δ | | bicĕ'-yaδ |
| turtle-neck | kawĭ'na-kŭ | kawĭ'na-ŭtca | kana'dihwa-kδĭ |
| turtle-back | kawĭ'na-tcĭdik | | kana'dihwa-kĭdĭ |
| goose-excrement | | | La'l-a-pa |
| grasshopper-elbow | cakδ'-bĭya | cakδ'-pĭya | |
| killdeer eyebrow | | kamtĭ'ltalĭ-ŭĭ kŭwĭ | |
| crow foot (or track) | kaa'i-kama | kaa'i-kama | |
| deer-elbow | | pcĕ'-pĭya | |
| sunfish-rib | | tsawa'l-msak | tsawa'l-mĭsak |
| mosquito | bita'mta | | |
| starfish | | stĕ'ik | |
| crab-claw | kĭ'-ʈana | | |
| turtle-foot | kawĭ'na-kama | kawĭ'na-kama | kana'dĭhwa-kama |
| bat's wing | kata'talak-ca | | |
| bear-foot (or track) | bita'-kama | | |
| deer-breast-? | bice'-yee-nat | | |
| deer-stand in | | | bicĕ'-tδ |
| elbow | bĭya' | katŭ'k, pĭya' | biya', bĭ'ya' |
| *Plants* | | | |
| potato-forehead | | | bŭ'-dile |
| acorn-head (or cup) | maa-ka'tδla | pdŭ-cna | |
| acorn | maa | | |
| pine-tree | kawa'ca | | |
| potato-forehead-eye | | | bŭ'-dilĕ-ŭĭ |

| Artificial | Northern | Central | Eastern |
|---|---|---|---|
| arrowhead | katca'k | katca' | kaga' |
| arrowhead-half | | katca'-dalaū | kaga'-daLaū |
| arrowhead-sharp | | katca-mset | kaga'-mĭset |
| arrowhead-slender | | katca'-mtil | |
| inward-arrowhead | | tca'l-katca | |
| outward-arrowhead | | ko'l-katca | |
| arrowhead-sharp pointed | | katca'-mtĭp | |
| arrow-split open | | | xaga'-mĭLaū |
| arrowhead-projecting | | | xaga'-dĭset |
| string | | ale'ma | |
| game (played with fish vertebrae) | datce'kka | | |
| stretcher | | | kaitsa'kai |
| | | | xaitsa'k |
| | | | xaitsa'kai |
| tattoo | ha'ske | | |
| star | | kaa'mūl | ūyahŏ' |

*Geometric*

| | | | |
|---|---|---|---|
| zigzag (by which is meant almost any crooked line or object) | tsīyŏ'tsīyŏ | tsīyŏ'tsīyŏ | tsīyŏ'tsīyŏ |
| | katīyŏ'tĭyŏ | ka't yŏtīyŏ | xatīyŏ'tĭyŏ |
| | tsīyŏ'tsīyŏka | tsīyŏ'tsīyŏka | dziyŏ'dziyŏka |
| | dzĭyŏdzīyŏ | | dziyŏdziyŏ' |
| | tsakŏ'kakŏka | | |
| | tsīkĕ'ga (?) | | |
| wavy | dīkŏ'tka | | |
| large spots, spots | dapŏ'kka | | |
| spotted | dapŏ'dapŏka | | dapŏ'kpŏkŏ |
| | dapŏ'kpŏkŏ | | kapŏ'kpŏkŏ |
| | dapŏ'dapŏ | | |
| | dīta'aka | | |
| spot or dot | dīta's | | dīta's |
| small figures | dapĭ'dapīka | | |
| | sisī'sīsī | | |
| | dapĭ'dapĭ | | |
| little-pieces | bĭyŏ'bĭyŏ | | |
| | bĭyŏ'bĭyŏka | | |

*Miscellaneous*

| | | | |
|---|---|---|---|
| initial design | caiyŏ'ĭ | caiyŏ'ĭ | caiyŏ'ĭ |
| finishing design | baiya'kaū | baiya'kaū | hĭ'baiyax |
| empty | kata' | | |
| east-this-mark | | | cŏ'-bax-kama |
| east-place-from-mark | | cŏ-ma-ke'kama | |
| daylight (?) | | kaa' | |
| door | da'ū, hamaka'm | ham, ha'mda | hwa |

| Modern | Northern | Central | Eastern |
|---|---|---|---|
| whiteman | masa'n | masa'n | masa'n |
| new | | cŭwĕ' | ciwĕ' |
| cross | | karŭ's | |
| cards (a game) | | wada'ha | |
| calico | | yanī'ya | |
| man (human being) | tca | tcatc | ka'ŭk |
| design | datŏ'ī | dītcī', tcī | |
| mark | kama' | kama' | kama', xama' |

Among these names there are two, elbow and daylight, which should be disregarded, as they are doubtful translations and do not appear to be logically connected with the designs to which they are applied. In that case the total number of design names in use would be fifty-two. In order to arrive at the total number of truly aboriginal names, six, which are due to white influence and classified here as modern design names, should be subtracted, thus leaving forty-eight aboriginal names.

So far as at present may be judged all·these names are of truly Pomo origin, there being no evidence now at hand of borrowing by the Pomo from other people. No positive statements can, however, be made upon this point until more knowledge is available about the basketry of the peoples occupying the territory surrounding that of the Pomo.

Not all these names are used by the people of all three Pomo divisions. There are ten pairs of names which may be considered as equivalents, as follows: deer-back and potato-forehead; turtle-neck and turtle-back; goose-excrement and finishing design; grasshopper-elbow and deer-elbow; zigzag and wavy; large-spots, spots, and spot or dot; small-figures and little-pieces; empty and arrowhead; east-this-mark and east-place-from-mark. The presence of these equivalent names accounts in part for what appears superficially as a radical difference in designs in passing from one of the Pomo divisions to another. Of fully equal importance also are the differences in the qualifying terms used in the different divisions and particularly the variations in the uses of these qualifying terms by different informants. In addition to these names which are equivalent in their application, there are in each of these divisions a number which are not used in either of the other divisions and which have no equivalents, so

that the total number of names used by any one division alone
is very much below fifty-two. In fact the largest number used
by any one of the divisions is thirty-five, that used by the Northern. The Central and Eastern have respectively thirty-two and
twenty-five. If from these be subtracted the names due to white
influence and introduced in modern times, the Northern would
have but thirty-three, the Central twenty-six, and the Eastern
twenty-two names of strictly aboriginal origin. From the second
number should be also subtracted the two doubtful names above
mentioned, these occurring only in that division, thus leaving the
total for the Central division only twenty-four.

Among these names there are many which are rarely met
with. The number in common use among all three of the divisions under consideration is but twenty-eight, and two of these
are names of modern origin, so that twenty-six truly aboriginal
names are the only ones applied to the majority of the designs.
Similarly each one of the divisions taken separately shows a comparatively small number of names in common use, the three
divisions having respectively twenty-one, nineteen, and sixteen
such names, of which one, two, and two respectively are names
of modern origin, leaving the total numbers of truly aboriginal
names in common use twenty, seventeen, and fourteen respectively for the three divisions.

A notable feature of these terms is the predominance of animal names. As is shown by the above mentioned table there are
in all three of the divisions taken together twenty-three animal
names of which twelve are in common use, this being three times
as great a number as is found in any of the other classes of names
and nearly one-half the total number of names commonly in use.
In the main these names denote parts of the various animals,
though some are simply names of the animate objects themselves.
There are sixteen names of animate objects, as follows: deer,
striped-watersnake, quail, ant, butterfly, turtle, goose, grasshopper, killdeer, crow, sunfish, mosquito, starfish, crab, bat, bear;
and twelve terms relating to parts of the body, as follows: back,
plume, teeth, neck, excrement, elbow, eyebrow, foot (or track),
rib, claw (or hand), wing, breast (?). To these last should be
added three other terms which appear in plant names, namely:

head, forehead, and eye, making a total of fifteen terms referring to parts of the body. The remaining names which are commonly in use have been here placed in four classes, in none of which however is there any considerable number. While the number of animal names commonly in use is twelve, the number of plant names commonly in use is but two, of artificial objects but four, of geometrical figures but four, and of miscellaneous objects but four, thus showing a very great predominance of animal names when compared with any one of the other classes.

As has already been shown, the various design elements are given names of special signification, such as names of animals, birds, plants, artificial objects, etc., but an inspection of the figures of the design elements and also of the patterns appearing in the plates will show that the designs to which these names are applied are not in most cases at all realistic. They are not intended by the Indians to be so, as is shown by their statements that they never attempted to represent realistically animals, trees, flowers, mountains, stars, thunder, lightning, etc. The Indians do not attach any realistic significance to them, except perhaps to the quail-plume design (figs. 211 to 222), which they assert really does look like the plume of the valley quail. It is also true that the Indians do not attach any religious significance to these figures. They are mainly decorative and seem in all cases to have been named from some real or fancied likeness to objects bearing the same names.

## QUALIFYING TERMS.

The figures and plates and their descriptions show that, while the Pomo have only a comparatively small number of elemental design names, the variation in form and proportions of the design elements to which these names are applied is very great. The lack of names of elements is, in a great measure, compensated by the use of qualifying terms, which assists in differentiating designs which are similar, yet quite distinct one from another. These qualifying terms, which are applied chiefly to elemental figures, though some of them are applied also to patterns, may be divided into seven general classes. There are seventeen terms relating to form, five to direction, three to position, three to size, four to color, five to number, and four to quality. There are also four terms of miscellaneous significance. The following table shows these terms and the particular dialectic divisions in which each is used.

## QUALIFYING TERMS USED WITH ELEMENTAL NAMES.

| Form | Northern | Central | Eastern |
|---|---|---|---|
| sharp | ditĭ'p, mĭse't | mset | ditĭ'p, mĭse't |
| slender | | mtil | |
| barbed | dase't | | dase't |
| sharp pointed, sharp point | datĭ'p | ŏ'pitai, mtĭp | datĭ'p |
| sharp points. | datĭ'pka | | |
| | kase'tka | | |
| projecting | | | dĭse't |
| pointed | dītĭ'pka | | |
| wide mark | | | dŭta'p |
| drawn out | kala'tkaŭ | kala'tkaŭ | |
| large area | data'pan | | data'p |
| | data'pka | | |
| split open | | | mĭLa'ŭ |
| forked | | | bana' |
| compressed | datsŭ'ttcĭka | | |
| long | | kasŭ'ltak | bagi'l |
| | | kŏ'lai | |
| short | | ptcŏ'yai | |
| circular, circle | tcada'mŭl | tcadŏ'tcadō | |
| globular | tcadŏ'lai | | |
| **Direction** | | | |
| inward | | tcal | |
| outward | | kol | |
| upward | ŭ'yŭl | | kaiyŭla'l |
| downward | yŏ'wil | | |
| from (?) | | ke (?) | |
| **Position** | | | |
| above | | naŭ | |
| lower | | yŏ | |
| pushed-over | dĭka'tka | | |
| **Size** | | | |
| big | | | tĭa |
| small | bitcŭ'tcai | | kŭt, kŭ'dja, |
| | | | xŭt |
| swelled or bulged | | katsŭ'ttci. | |

| Color | Northern | Central | Eastern |
|---|---|---|---|
| black | katse′ | | |
| white | kale′ | | |
| blank | | kalŭ′ | xaLŭ′ |

| Number | | | |
|---|---|---|---|
| half | | balaŭ, balaŭ-ai, dalaŭ | daLaŭ |
| both | xŏl | | xa′lĭ |
| one (or single) | | ta′tŭ | |
| three | | sĭ′bŏ | |
| eye-half | | ŭ′ĭ-balaŭ | |
| | | ŭĭ-balaŭ-ai | |

| Quality | | | |
|---|---|---|---|
| ugly (or imperfect) | | baset | |
| resembling | | ĭ′tcai | ĭ′tcai |
| nothing | | | xale′l |
| foolish (or nonsensical) | | | dagŏ′l |

| Miscellaneous | | | |
|---|---|---|---|
| coiled-basket | | ctŭ | |
| throw | nĕ′tak | | |
| stir (?) | | | dabe′l |
| rub (?) | dana′ | | |

Some of these terms are applicable to any and all design elements, while others are used only in connection with one or two. For instance, inward, outward, above, lower, slender, and sharp are used only with arrowhead. Further, many of these terms are used by the people of all three of the Pomo divisions investigated, while others are restricted to perhaps a single division. For instance, the terms inward, outward, above, and lower when used as qualifiers of names of elements, are employed only by the Central Pomo.

These qualifying terms show a predominance of terms relating to form, there being seventeen of them. This is to be explained by the fact that they are applied in most cases to single figures, not to combinations of figures as are the qualifying terms relating to patterns. The small numbers of terms of direction and of position are noticeable, but are to be expected by virtue of the fact that terms of these two classes belong logically with patterns or the combinations of two or more figures.

# PATTERN NAMES.

Names of patterns, as has already been shown, are combinations of the names of their constituent elements, together with appropriate qualifying terms. In a great measure these pattern names are constant and uniform within the limits of any one of the Pomo divisions, so that the same phrase-name, consisting of the accepted names of the constituent elemental figures and the appropriate qualifying terms, is given in connection with any particular pattern by all informants speaking the same dialect. There are, however, very considerable differences in these phrase-names within the same dialectic area, due to the individual conception of the form or size of the design elements which go to make up the pattern as a whole. For instance, one informant might consider the small rectangles which form part of a pattern as of sufficient size to be called deer-back, while another might consider them so small as to require the designation of ants. Another source of variety in these phrase-names and one which is responsible for fully as great variation as this difference in individual interpretation of form or size of the elemental figures themselves, is the difference in the use of qualifying terms, of which there are a large number.

## QUALIFYING TERMS.

Just as the greater number of qualifying terms used in connection with design elements are naturally descriptive of form, owing to the fact that the elemental designs are in most cases single figures, so the qualifying terms used particularly in connection with pattern names are indicative of relative position and spatial relations owing to the different combinations of elemental figures which go to make up the patterns. The differentiation of patterns depends largely upon the relative position and spatial relations in which the constituent elements stand one to another. As is shown in the following table, there are thirty-four of these terms giving these relations, and also mentioning the several methods of patterns arrangement employed by the Pomo. Some of these terms are used by the people of but one of the Pomo divisions, while others are used by the people of all three divisions. Those most commonly occurring are crossing, in-the-middle, in-the-center, on-both-sides, collected, placed-close-together-in-a-row, and (in addition to) side, and on.

In addition to this large number of terms relating to position there are also qualifying terms relating to form and direction, there being five terms in each of these classes. Of these the terms band, broad-band, striped, and lead occur most frequently.

### QUALIFYING TERMS USED WITH PATTERN NAMES.

| Position | Northern | Central | Eastern |
|---|---|---|---|
| crossing | dase'tka<br>minadatē'kama<br>minadatēkamū | ūna'Liū | wīna'līhempke |
| crossed | dise'tka | | |
| one on top of another | batcō'tama | | |
| in the middle | dilē' | la'la | dilē' |
| in the center | | lē'Lan | |
| on both sides | xō'l-tū | | kō''nawa<br>xō''nawa |
| following on the outside | | kōwaldakade'n<br>kōwaldakadē'tan | |
| on the outside | | kō'wal | |
| running along in pairs | | | xōtca'gan |
| going around | | | kadabe'mlī |
| going around and meeting | tcadī'mul<br>tcacīte'mūl | | |
| meet | daiye'kamū<br>daiye'tkamū | | kōldaiyaū'hmak<br>xōldabē'hmak |
| collect, collected | daie'n | | |
| connected | | cte'ltele | |
| interlocking | kate'ltaimaū | | gaūcaiya'ūhmak |
| together | | katcō'm | |
| tied together | | | pase'r |
| placed close together in a row | daie'nga | | |
| scattered along in a line | dakīkīti'nka<br>dasē'sētenka | | |
| scattered around in a circle | dasī'dasī-mūl | | |
| scattered along | dakīkītin | | |
| scattered around | daki'tka<br>dasī'dasī | | |
| scattered | dasī'dasi<br>dasī'dasīka | mka'lītcai | |
| separated | | kata'iitcai | |
| far-apart (?) | | taka'nma | |

| along | | | dai |
|---|---|---|---|
| above, upper | ŭ'yŭ | | |
| close | kana' | | |
| near | | mala'da | |
| among | | | xam |
| side | tŭ | tŭl | |
| stuck-on | | tcil, tci'ltaŭ | |
| on | | tŏl | |
| and (or with) | | | hua, na |

*Form*

| band | | ctot | lik |
|---|---|---|---|
| broad band | datsai'-banem | | |
| straight band | cīte'n | | |
| stripe | cīke't, cīke'tka | tcūwa'k | |
| | | tcūwa'n | |
| straight line (or lines) | cīte' | | |

*Direction*

| passing along | date'n | | gadi'l |
|---|---|---|---|
| running along | | | gīwa'l |
| extending, extended | cīkīkīti'nka | | |
| follow up | | kade'n | |
| | | kadē'tan | |
| lead | cīde'n | | cūdi'l |

As has already been shown, the number of names of elemental designs in common use among the Pomo when compared to the number of elements themselves is comparatively small. In all three of the Pomo divisions under consideration there are twenty-six truly aboriginal names in common use, and in any one of these divisions alone the number of such names does not exceed twelve. However, by combining the names of all or, at least, most of the elements in a complex pattern and by adding appropriate qualifying terms, the Pomo are able to produce descriptive phrase-names, by which they can adequately differentiate the most complex patterns. As before stated, however, these descriptive phrase-names differ to a certain extent according to the interpretation which the individual informant puts upon the various elements constituting the pattern and to the individual's conception of the relation in which these elements stand, one to another.

When compared with the design names found among certain other California peoples the Pomo have a large number, probably due both to linguistic diversity and variety of environment.

In the previous pages the names in use by three of the seven Pomo divisions only have been given, those of the other four divisions not being now available. While the people of these three dialectic divisions are quite closely related the differences between any two are very considerable, even amounting in some features of their speech to a true language rather than a dialectic difference. Under such conditions the people of any one of these divisions might from time to time modify a name held in common by all three, originate a new name, or allow one of the old ones to fall into disuse. In any of these cases the differences in language and the consequent difficulties of communication among the people would make the changed or new term slow to spread from one division to another. This difficulty of transmission would be still greater if the whole seven Pomo dialects, some of which are much more remotely connected one to another than the three considered, be taken into account. If the design names used by the people of all seven of the Pomo divisions were available it is probable that the present number, forty-eight, of truly aboriginal names would be increased, possibly as much as fifty per cent.

There are also very considerable differences in the topography and in the environmental conditions existing in different parts of the territory occupied by these three divisions of the Pomo. Their territory extends from the ocean to the crest of the inner or main range of the Coast Range mountains, and covers four distinct topographical zones, as has been pointed out in treating the topography of this region.* Under these conditions it is to be expected that the basket designs would be considerably affected, as is the case with various other important features of culture. Combining then these differences of natural environment with the linguistic diversity, conditions are given under which it is to be expected that a considerable number of design names would arise, and it is natural that the Pomo should have fully as great a number of elemental names as any other people inhabiting a like territory.

An inspection of the region inhabited by the Yurok, Karok,

---

* The Ethno-Geography of the Pomo and Neighboring Indians, Univ. Cal. Publ. Arch. Ethn., VI, 8, 1908.

and Hupa and of that inhabited by the Maidu is interesting in this connection. The former may here be considered together for, while they differ entirely in language, they live in contiguous territories and are a unit in culture. Their territory does not show so great diversity of environment as that of the Pomo but in their language they, like the Pomo, are in three groups. While lexically these languages are entirely different the peoples themselves mingled freely. In this respect, therefore, they are similar to the three Pomo divisions under consideration and like them collectively possess somewhere between forty and fifty design names.

The Maidu occupied a territory much larger than that of the three Pomo divisions and also much larger than that held by the three Northwestern peoples. They also are divided linguistically into three dialectic groups and their territory like that of the Pomo shows considerable diversity of topography and environment, since it extends from the broad plain of the Sacramento valley to the high Sierras. These great differences of elevation, with consequent differences of temperature, flora, and fauna, gave rise to an environment which, like that of the three Pomo divisions, is very diverse and must have influenced design names and other matters of culture to an appreciable extent. It is therefore not surprising that among the Maidu also there are in use something over forty design names.

Thus among the representatives of the three culture groups, the three Northwestern peoples, the Maidu, and the Pomo, concerning whose basketry there is information now available, and among whom the conditions of linguistic and environmental diversity are, to a considerable extent at least, comparable, the numbers of basket design names seem to be about equal and to range between forty and fifty.

In general, therefore, it appears that the Pomo possess fully as great a number of elemental names as do the Indians inhabiting any other territory of like extent, and it seems probable that the number is considerably greater than that to be found among other peoples with equal or greater territory but with more uniform environmental conditions and with less diversity of language.

# CONCLUSION.

The fiber materials employed by the Pomo in their basketry are, with the exception of the bark of the redbud, taken from the roots of such plants as the sedge, carex, and pine. For the foundation material in coiling and for warp in twining the slender stems of the willow are almost exclusively used, those of the hazel being employed only in the extreme northern part of the Pomo region.

The use of feathers and beads in the ornamentation of Pomo basketry is one of its most characteristic features. The feathers are employed either for outlining designs which appear in fiber, or making the designs themselves. In the latter case the entire surface of the basket is thickly covered in such a manner that the background and pattern are brought out by the different colored feathers instead of by the fiber.

In technique Pomo basketry is characterized by great variety. Three different types, coiling, twining, and wickerwork, are found. Of coiling there are two forms, single-rod and three-rod; of twining there are seven, plain, diagonal, lattice, and two forms of three-strand twining, and two forms of three-strand braiding. While most other California peoples use one type of technique almost exclusively, the Pomo alone to a slight extent make use of wickerwork and employ very extensively both twining and coiling.

The forms also of Pomo baskets show great range. They vary in shape from the very flat plate-form to almost perfect spheres and to cones of various proportions. In addition to these a special elliptical or boat-shaped basket, a form rarely met with elsewhere, is quite frequently made by them.

The variety of pattern arrangements found among the Pomo is very striking. The predominating arrangement, especially upon twined baskets, is horizontal or banded. A considerable proportion of the baskets have their patterns placed diagonally. Comparatively few have patterns arranged so they cross one another, or so as to cover the entire surface of the basket in the manner shown in pl. 16, fig. 6. A very few coiled baskets have a vertical or an individual arrangement of their patterns.

Symmetry in the disposition of the patterns is to a large extent lacking.   Not only is there no such careful balancing of the parts of the horizontal patterns as is found in Northwestern California, but even such banded patterns possess a break in their continuity. This may be either very small or of considerable size and filled with a design quite different from that of the remainder of the pattern.   Obviously no symmetry is possible in the crossing and individual arrangements.   In the diagonal and vertical arrangements, however, the patterns are so placed at three or four equidistant points as to be symmetrical.

The ornamentation of Pomo basketry consists of a great number of complex and varied patterns each composed of simple design elements, such as lines, triangles, rectangles, rhomboids, etc. By various modifications of these simple elements a large number of forms of any one class are available for combination to make the complex patterns.   By repeating a single element, or, as is more often the case, by combining several, a very elaborate pattern may be produced.

Similarly, the names applied to design elements and to patterns are of two different kinds.   The former are simple terms derived from the names of animals, plants, artificial objects, etc. and are given by reason of some real or fancied likeness of the design to the object bearing the name.   These simple names are qualified by various terms descriptive of form, size, position, color, etc. so as to be fairly exact designations.   As patterns are formed by combining various design elements, pattern names result from the combination of the names of the various elements concerned.   By means of additional qualifying terms the relation in which these various elements stand to one another is indicated.

It is thus not only possible to adequately differentiate the most complex patterns one from the other, but by this combination of element names and qualifying terms pattern phrase-names result which are so descriptive that it is possible for anyone acquainted with the subject to form a mental picture of the pattern from its name.

To these elaborate patterns composed of simple, largely geometrical elements, provided with purely descriptive names based upon some real or fancied likeness to objects bearing the same names, the Indians do not attach any religious or symbolic significance.

# GLOSSARY.*

ai, plural suffix used with adjectives (N, C).

badjŏ' tule (N).

bagi'l, long (E).

bag'ŏ', tule (E).

ba'iya-hakŏ, cylindrical fish-trap (C).

baiya'kau, finishing design. Also used in speaking of long stitches such as basting of cloth or in basketry, twining which covers two or more warp sticks like that about the rims of the baskets shown in pl. 21 (N, C).

bala'ŭ, half (C).

bala'ŭ-ai, half [plural] (C).

bam, willow stem (N).

bam-sa'i, diagonal twining (C).

ba'm-sūbŭ, three-rod foundation (N).

ba'm-tca, single-rod foundation (N).

bam-tŭc', plain twining (N, C, E).

bana', forked (E).

bane'm, to set down or place an object (N).

base't, ugly [or imperfect] (C).

batcŏ', tule (C).

batcŏ'tama, one-on-top-of-another (N).

bati, hazel (N).

bati'bŏom, hemispherical basket (N).

bati'lmahwak, ? (E).

batŏ', basketry seed-beater (E).

batsĭ'ya, yellowhammer (N).

batŭ', basketry seed-beater N, C).

bax, this (E).

bicĕ', deer (N, E).

bicĕ'-maŏ, deer-back (N, E).

bicĕ'-ŏ, deer-teeth (N).

bicĕ'-to, deer-stand-in (E).

bicĕ'-yaŏ, deer-teeth (E).

bicĕ'-yee-nat, deer-breast-? (N).

bidjĭ', burden basket [closely woven] (N).

bilĭ'ya, red-winged blackbird (N).

bis-yem, bracken, a black basket material (N).

bita', bear (N).

bita'-kama, bear-foot [or track] (N).

bita'mta, mosquito (N).

bitcŭ'tcai, small [plural] (N).

bito'i-tsoi, burden basket [openwork of peeled rods] (N).

bitsŭ'l, small openwork storage basket (E).

---

* The alphabet used in this glossary is described in the present series of publications, VI, 51, 1908 (Ethno-Geography of the Pomo Indians).

bitŭm'tu, ant (N).

bīya', elbow (N).

bī'ya', elbow (E).

bīyŏ'bīyŏ, little pieces (N).

bīyŏ'bīyŏka, little-pieces (N).

bŭ, "Indian potatoes," by which is meant the bulbs, corms, and tubers
  of the various species of bulbous and tubrous rooted plants in
  which the Pomo region abounds (E).

bŭ'-dile, potato-forehead. [According to some informants this term refers to a protuberance on the upper surface of certain bulbs and
  corms called "Indian potatoes." Some other informants claim
  that the reference is to a protuberance on the under surface of these
  "Indian potatoes."] (E).

bŭ'-dile ŭī, potato-forehead eye (E).

bŭgŭ', burden basket [closely woven] (E).

bŭka'l, conical fish-trap (N).

bŭm, starting knots used in twined basketry (N, C).

bŭxa'l, conical fish-trap (E).

ca, arm [or wing] (N).

ca'di, basket (E).

caga'ga, quail (E).

caga'ga-ke, quail-plume (E).

caga'ga-xe, quail-plume (E).

cag'a'x, quail (E).

cag'a'x-hakŏi, quail-trap (E).

cag'a'x-ke, quail-plume (E).

cag'a'x-xe, quail-plume (E).

caiyŏ'ī, inital design (N, C, E).

caka'ga, quail (N, C, E).

caka'ga-hakŏi, quail-trap (N, C).

caka'ga-ke, quail-plume (E).

caka'ga-kĕya, quail-plume (N, C).

caka'ga-xe, quail-plume (E).

caka'ka, quail (N, C).

caka'ka-kĕya, quail-plume (N, C).

caka'n, openwork basket [culinary type] (N).

caka'n-tīn, openwork basket [sifter type] (N).

cakŏ', grasshopper (N, C).

cakŏ -bīya, grasshopper-elbow (N).

cakŏ'-pīya, grasshopper-elbow (C).

cala'p, openwork basket [sifter type] (E).

ca'-mīdje, truncated cone fish-trap (E).

ca'-mtce, truncated cone fish-trap (C).

cat, basket (E).

ca'tanī, shell beads (E).

catco'm, juniper (?) root, a white basket material (C).

cate'p, juniper (?) root, a white basket material (E).

cbŭ, coiling (C).

cee't, twining (C);
>    cylindrical basket [small] (C).

cee't-tcibūtcibū, spherical basket (C).

cibū', coiling (N).

cĭde'n, lead [verb] (N).

cĭke't, stripe (N).

cĭke'tka, stripe (N).

cĭkĭkĭtin'ka, extending, extended. Applied to anything drawn out or
>    strung out for a great distance; also to anything unraveled (N).

cĭl, lark (C).

cĭlō', elliptical or boat-shaped basket (N).

cĭte', straight line; straight lines (N).

cĭte'n, straight band (N).

cĭtsĭn', three-strand twining; three-strand braiding (N).

ciwĕ', new (E).

cĭyi'n, grape-vine, a binding material (N).

cna, head (C).

cŏ, east (C, E).

cŏ'bax-kama, east-this-mark. A name applied by the Eastern Pomo to
>    certain patterns said by some to have been introduced into their
>    basketry from that of the people living to the east of them.

cŏ'-ma, east-place (C).

cŏ-ma ke'kama, east-place from mark (C).

ctel'tele, connected, hitched together (C).

cti'n, grape-vine, a binding material (C, E).

ctot, band (C).

ctū, coiling (C);
>    coiled-basket (C);
>    hemispherical basket (C).

ctū'-ptcĭ, basket of truncated cone form (C).

cūdi'l, lead [verb] (E).

cūsa's, diagonal twining (E).

cūse't, diagonal twining (N).

cūw'ĕ, new (C).

cūwĭ'rĭ, three-strand twining; three-strand braiding (E).

cwi'tki, three-strand twining; three-strand braiding (C).

dabe'l, stir (?) (E).

dagal, ? (E).

dago'l, foolish [or nonsensical] (E).

dai, along (E).

daie'n, collect; collected (N).

daie'nga, placed close together in a row. [When used in reference to
>    design.] In general, to collect a number of objects together in one
>    place (N).

daiye'kamū, meet [singular] (N).

daiye'tkamū, meet [plural] (N).

dakĭ'kĭtin, scattered along; moving along (N).

dakĭkĭti'nka, scattered along in a line (N).

daki'tka, scattered around (N).

dako', willow hoop (C).

dakŏ', willow hoop (N, E).

dala', plate-form basket (N, E).

dala'kan, plate-form basket [small] (N).

dala'ŭ, half (C).

daLa'ŭ, half (E).

dana', rub (?) (N).

dapĭ'dapĭ, small-figures (N).

dapĭ'dapĭka, small-figures (N).

dapŏ'dapŏ, spotted (N).

dapŏ'dapŏka, spotted (N).

dapŏ'kka, large spots, particularly if they are at considerable distances from one another (N).

dapŏ'kpoka, spotted (N).

dapŏ'kpŏko, spotted (N, C).

dasĕ'sĕtenka, scattered along in a line (N).

dase't, barbed; sharp points [two or more points] (N, E).

dase'tka, crossing (N).

dasĭ'dasĭ, scattered or scattered around (N).

dasĭ'dasĭka, scattered [either promiscuously or in a row] (N).

dasĭ'dasĭ-mŭl, scattered around in a circle (N).

data'p, large area; wide mark (E).

data'pan, large area (N).

datapka, large area [of any shape] (N).

datcĕ'datcenka, ? (N).

datce'kka, the name of a game in which a wooden or other skewer is thrust through as many as possible of a string of fish vertebrae as the string is passing through the air.

datĕkama, lie-on.

date'n, passing along (plural).

datĭ'p, sharp point; sharp-pointed (N, E).

datĭ'pka, sharp points (N).

datŏ'ĭ, design (N);
      mark of any kind (N).

datsa'i, broad (N).

datsa'i-banem, broad-band. Literally broad placed or put on. It is used in reference to certain basket designs and is equivalent to broad band (N).

datsŭ'tka, ? (N).

datsŭ'ttcika, compressed. Strictly the compressing or squeezing of any soft material (N).

daŭ, space or opening in a pattern, literally door.

dem, cylindrical basket [small] (N).

dĭka'tka, pushed over (N).

dikŏ'tka, wavy (N).

dilĕ', forehead; in-the-middle (N, E).

dĭsa'i, redbud, a red basket material (E).

disai-tŏ'ts, redbud, a white basket material (E).

dīse't, projecting; applied to any objects which stick up or project prominently (C,E).

dīse'ta, crossed (N).

dīta's, dot, spot, daub (N, E).

dītas'ka, spotted or daubed more than once (N).

dītcī', design (C).

dītī'p, sharp (N, E).

dītī'pka, pointed (N).

dīti'r, openwork storage basket (E).

djama', twining; wickerwork (?) (N).

djicī'l, lark (N).

dŭka'l, wickerwork (E).

dŭta'p, wide mark; large area (E).

dsīyo'dsīyŏ, zigzag (N, E).

dsīyŏ'dsīyŏka, zigzag (E).

gadi'l, passing along (E).

gai, ? (E).

gaiī'-ce, willow root, a white basket material (E).

ga'iya, ? (E).

gaŭcaiya'ŭhmak, interlocking (E).

gīca'l, tule (N).

gīwa'l, running along (E).

gūca'l, tule (E).

gūcī'li, lark (E).

gūmŭ'Lŭ, spherical basket (E).

ha'i-dŭkal, burden basket [openwork of unpeeled rods] (N).

hainĕ'dŭ, lattice twining (C).

hai-sī'bo, three-rod foundation (C).

ha'i-tatu, single-rod foundation (C).

ha'kŏ, conical fish-trap (C).

ha'l-tsawam, border-weave (or braid), literally toward (or at) the mouth braid (C).

ham, space or opening in a pattern, literally end; also near the mouth [used in reference to finishing designs and weaves] (C).

ha'mda, space or opening in a pattern, literally end of it (C).

hamaka'm, finishing design (N).

ha'ake, tattoo [refers to tattoo marks] (N).

hī'baiyax, finishing design (E).

hna, and [or with] (E).

hwa, space or opening in a pattern, literally door (E).

īka'l, burden basket [openwork of peeled rods] (C).

ī'-pīka, feathered basket (N).

i'tcai, resemble, looks like (C, E).

itī't, openwork storage basket; wickerwork (?) (C).

kaa', daylight (?) (C).

kaa'i, crow (C).

kaa'i-kama, crow foot [or track] (N, C).

kaa'mŭl, star (C).

kaca'icai, butterfly (N, C, E).

kacĭ'ltsiya, bluebird (E).

kadabe'mli, going around [plural] (E).

kade'n, follow up (C).

kadĕ'tan, follow up [plural] (C).

kadĭ'-kūhŭm, sedge, a white basket material (N).

kaga', arrowhead (E).

kaga'-daLaŭ, arrowhead-half (E).

kaga'-mĭset, arrowhead-sharp (E).

ka'ia, shell beads (N).

kaia'n, mallard (N, C, E).

kaitsa'kai, stretcher [see xaitsa'k] (E).

kaiyŏ'ĭ, oriole (C).

kaiyŏ'yŭ, oriole (N).

kaiyūla'l, upward (E).

kakaiûtcŏ'm, ? (C).

ka'kŏi, cylindrical fish-trap (N).

kala'cŭna, elliptical or boat-shaped basket (C).

kala'ia, redbud, a red basket material (C).

kala'ia-katŏ, redbud, a white basket material (C).

kala'l, willow stem (N, C).

kala'l-sĭbo, three-rod foundation (C).

kala'l-yem, willow root, a white basket material (N).

kala't, approximately parallel lines (C).

kala'tkaŭ, drawn-out (N, C).

kale', white (N).

kale'-ce, digger-pine root, a white basket material (N, C, E).

kale'l, nothing (E).

kalĭtcŏ'tco, bluebird (N).

kalŭ', blank, space (C).

kalŭ'tŭduk, striped-watersnake (E).

kalŭ'tŭruk, striped-watersnake (E).

kama, mark; foot [or track] (N, C, E).

ka'mtiltali, killdeer (C).

kamtĭ'ltalĭ-ûĭ-kûwĭ, killdeer-eyebrow (C).

kana', close (N).

kana'dĭhwa, turtle (E).

kana'dĭhwa-kama, turtle-foot (E).

kana'dĭhwa-kĭdĭ, turtle-back (E).

kana'dĭhwa-kŏĭ, turtle-neck (E).

kapŏ'kpŏkŏ, spotted (C).

kara'tc, redheaded woodpecker (E).

karŭ's, cross [derived from the Spanish cruz] (C).

kase'tka, sharp-points (N).

kasŭl'tak, long (C).

kata', empty, blank, nothing (N).

kata'iitcai, separated [plural] (?); set-far-apart [plural] (?) (C).

kata'k, redheaded woodpecker (C).

kata'talak, bat (N).

kata'talak-ca, bat's wing (N).

kata'tc, redheaded woodpecker (N).

katca', arrowhead; also applied to the obsidian knife (C).

katca'-dalaŭ, arrowhead-half (C).

katca'k, arrowhead (N).

katca'-mset, arrowhead-sharp (C).

katca'-mtil, arrowhead-slender (C).

katca'-mtĭp, arrowhead-sharp-pointed (C).

katcŏ'm, together (C).

kate'ltaimaŭ, interlocking (N).

ka'tĭyŏtĭyŏ, zigzag (N, C, E).

katĭ'yŏ'tĭ'yŏ, zigzag (C, E.)

ka'tŏla, cup (of acorn).

katsa'-kŭhŭm, sedge, a white basket material (E).

katse', black (N).

katsĭ'ya, yellowhammer (C).

ka'tsĭyŏtsĭyŏ, zigzag (N).

katsŭ'ttciŭ, swelled (C).

katū'k, elbow? (C).

kawa'ca, pine-tree (N).

kawĭn'a, turtle (N, C).

kawĭ'na-kama, turtle-foot (N, C).

kawĭ'na-kŭ, turtle-neck (N).

kawĭ'na-tcĭdik, turtle-back (N).

kawĭ'na-utca, turtle-neck (C).

ke, from (C).

kĕ'ya, plume or crest. Used in reference to the plume of the quail (N).

kĭ, crab (N).

kibŭ'k, coiling (E).

kĭ'cki, twining (E).

kĭdĭ, back, spinal column (E).

kĭ'-tana, crab claw [or hand] (N).

kohŏ'ĭ, mountain quail (N, C).

kŏ'ĭ, neck (E).

kol, outward. Used only in connection with such triangular elements as those shown in figs. 18 and 19, and said to signify that in making such a figure the work progresses constantly outward, *i.e.*, away from the middle of the pattern, by virtue of the fact that each row of twining is a little longer than the one next below. Cf. tcal (C).

kŏ'lai, long [plural] (C).

kŏldaiya'ŭhmak, meet (E).

kŏ'ĭ-katca, outward-arrowhead (C).

kŏ''nawa, on-both-sides (E).

kŏwal, on-the-outside (C).

kŏwaldakade'n, following on the outside (C).

kŏwaldakadĕ'tan, following on the outside [plural] (C).

kŭ, neck (N).

kŭ'dja, small (E).

kŭhŭm', sedge, a white basket material (N, C, E).

kŭt, small (E).

kŭ′ta, small (E).

Lal, goose (E).

la′la, middle, in-the-middle, among (C).

La′l-a-pa, goose excrement (E).

lĕ′Lan, center [geometric]; in-the-center (C).

li′bītsits, bracken, a black basket material (E).

lik, band (E).

maa′, acorn (N).

maa-ka′tŏla, acorn-head [or cup] (N).

ma′-ce, willow root, a white basket material (C).

mala′da, near (C).

maŏ′, back (N).

mao′dŏ-kit, bracken, a black basket material (C).

masa′kalak, striped-watersnake (N).

masa′n, whiteman (N, C, E).

ma′-yem, willow root, a white basket material (N).

meŏ′, back (C).

mīdje′, mortar basket (N, E).

mīLa′ū, split-open (E).

mille′, redbud, a red basket material (N).

mille-to′i, redbud, a white basket material (N).

mina′, over, upon (N).

mina′-datĕkama, crossing, literally top-lie-on  (N).

mina′datĕkama, crossing.  This term appears to differ from nina′datĕ-
     kama in that it carries a plural idea, that of crossing endlessly (N).

mīsa′k, rib (E).

mīsa′kala, striped-watersnake (N).

misa′kalak, striped-watersnake (N).

mīse′t, sharp (N, E).

mka′litcai, scattered [plural] (N).

msak, rib (C).

msa′kale, striped-watersnake (C).

mest, sharp (C).

mtca′kŏlai, ? (C).

mtce, mortar basket (C).

mtil, slender (C).

mtīp, sharp-pointed (C).

mto′t, border finish (C).

mŭl, in a circle, circular (N).

na, and [or with] (E).

nasū′, plate-form basket (C).

nat, ? (N).

naŭ, above (C).

nĕ′tak, throw.  Probably denotes long or extended (N).

o, teeth.  Applied not only to teeth but also to anything with a sharp
     edge or point (N, C).

ŏn′ma, basket (C).

ŏ′pitai, sharp-pointed (plural).

pa, excrement (E).

pase', openwork storage basket (N).

pase'r, tied-together, tied together in a bunch (E).

pce, deer (C).

pce'-með, deer-back (C).

pcĕ'-pīya, deer-elbow (C).

pdŭ, acorn (C).

pdŭ'-cna, acorn-head [or cup] (C).

pīka', basket (N).

pīka'-tcadŏl, spherical basket (N).

pīya', elbow (C).

po, magnesite beads (N, C).

pol, magnesite beads (E).

ptcī', burden basket [closely woven] (C).

ptcŏ'yai, short [plural] (C).

ptsat, starting knots used intwined basketry (C).

sal, openwork basket, culinary (C).

sa'l-stin, openwork basket [sifter type] (C).

sī'bŏ, three (C).

sīka, basketry cradle (N).

sīlī', starting knots used in twined basketry (N).

sīli'x, starting knots used in twined basketry (E).

sisi'sisi, small figures (N).

sī'wa, mountain robin (N, C, E).

sle'ma, string (C).

stĕ'ik, starfish (C).

sŭ'kan, plate-form sifting basket (C).

tacīma, redbud, a white basket material (E).

ta'kan, cylindrical basket (C).

taka'nma, far apart (?) (C).

talĕ'ya, shell beads (C).

tana', hand, claw (N).

ta'-pīka, feathered basket (N).

ta-sī'tŏi, feathered basket (E).

ta'-stŏl, feathered basket (C).

ta-tsaka't, bluebird (C).

ta'tŭ, one [or single] (C).

tcacdi'mŭl, going around and meeting [singular] (N).

tcacī'temŭl, going around and meeting [plural] (N).

tcada'mŭl, circle, circular (N).

tca'dim, ? (E).

tcadŏ'lai, globular [plural] (N).

tcadŏ'tcadŏ, circular (C).

tcal, inward, toward. Used only in connection with triangular elements such as those shown in figs. 17 and 20, and signifying that in making such a figure the work constantly progresses inward toward the middle of the pattern, by virtue of the fact that each row of twining fibers is a little shorter than the one next below. Cf. kol. (C).

tcal-katca, inward-arrowhead (C).

tcama'ŭ, twining; burden basket [openwork of unpeeled rods] (C).

tcĭ, design, mark, figure (C).

tcĭdi'k, back (N).

tcĭdĭ'yemūl, ? (N).

tcĭga', lattice-twining (E).

tcil, stuck on, hanging or stuck on the side or bottom (C).

tcĭ'yaŭ, ? (C).

tcūwa'k, stripe (C).

tcūwa'n, stripe (C).

te'm-gata, abalone shell (N).

tē'ŭ, plate-form basket [small] (C, E).

t!i', lattice-twining (N).

ti'a, big (E).

tirĭ'-bugu, basket of truncated cone form (E).

tĭya'l, yellowhammer (E).

tŏ, stand in (E).

tŏl, on (C).

too'-pĭka, cylindrical basket (N).

tsai, jay (N, C, E); single-rod foundation (N, C, E).

tsada'r, half-cylinder fish-trap (E).

tsada't, half-cylinder fish-trap (C).

tsaga'tsagaŭ, oriole (E).

tsakŏ'tsakŏka, zigzag (N).

tsatŏ'tŏ, robin (C).

tsawa'l, sunfish (C, E).

tsawa'l-mĭsak, sunfish-rib (E).

tsawa'l-msak, sunfish-rib (C).

tsawa'm, border finish, literally braid (N, C).

tsawa'mk, border finish, literally braid (E).

tsĭkē'ga, zigzag (?) (N).

tsilĭ', redwinged blackbird (C).

tsĭtŏk'tok, robin (N).

tsĭtŏ'tŏ, robin (E).

tsĭwi'c, balrush, a black basket material (N, C, E).

tsĭyŏ'tsĭyŏ, zigzag (N, C, E).

tsĭyŏ'tsiyŏka, zigzag (N, C).

tso'i, small openwork storage basket; burden basket [openwork of peeled
        or unpeeled rods] (N, E).

tsŭba'ha, willow stem (E).

tsŭhŭ'n, ? (N).

tsŭ'Lĭ, redwinged blackbird (E).

tŭ, side (N).

tŭ'ga, lattice-twining (E).

tŭl, side (C).

tŭ'ntŭn, ants (C, E).

ŭ'ĭ, eye (C, E).

u'ĭ-balaŭ, eye-half (C).

ŭ'ĭ-balaŭ-ai, eye-half [plural] (C).

ŭ'ĭ-kŭwĭ, eyebrow (C).

ŭna'Liŭ, crossing (C).

ŭtca', neck (C).

ŭyahŏ', star (E).

ŭyĭl'-to, basket of truncated cone form (N).

ŭ'yŭ, above, upper, up (C).

ŭ'yŭl, upward (N).

wada'ha, the Spanish game of cards (C).

wĭl, abalone shell (C).

wĭna', top, over (E).

wĭna'lĭhempke, crossing (E).

xaca'icai, butterfly (E).

xaga', arrowhead (E).

xaga'-dĭset, arrowhead projecting (E).

xaga'-miLaŭ, arrowhead-split-open (E).

xa'ĭ-kalĭ, single-rod foundation (E).

xa'ĭ-katŏli, basketry cradle (E).

xaitsa'k, a stretcher made by twining green withes together and used for carrying an injured person, as for instance one injured while hunting at a distance from the village (E).

xaitsa'kai, stretcher (E).

xai-xa'lĭ, plain twining (E).

xai-xŏ'mka, three-rod foundation (E).

xala'cŭna, elliptical or boat-shaped basket (E).

xale'l, nothing (E).

xa'lĭ, one [or single] (E).

xaLŭ', blank, space (E).

xam, among (E).

xama', mark, foot, track (E).

xana'dihwa, turtle (E).

xa'tĭyŏtĭyŏ, zigzag (E).

xatĭ'yŏ'tĭ'yŏ, zigzag (E).

xa'xŏi, cylindrical fish-trap (E).

xe, plume or crest, used in reference to the plume of the quail (E).

xŏl, both (N).

xŏ'ldabē'hmak, meet (E).

xŏ'l-tŭ, on-both-sides (N).

xŏ''nawa, on both sides (E).

xŏtca'gan, running along in pairs (E).

xŭt, small (E).

yanĭ'ya, calico (a term derived from the Spanish).

yaŏ, teeth (E).

yee, breast (N).

yĭl'-cat, feathered basket (E).

yŏ, lower, down (C).

yŏ'wĭl, downward (N).

## EXPLANATION OF PLATE 15.

Figure 1.—Starting knot with two pairs of warp sticks crossed and the weft elements passing diagonally to the angles formed.

Figure 2.—Starting knot with weft elements forming a cross with arms parallel to the warp sticks.

Figure 3.—Starting knot with no other fastening than the ordinary twining.

Figure 4.—Starting knot having two pairs on the outside and one pair inside.

Figure 5.—Starting knot with four warp sticks in each direction.

Figure 6.—Starting knot with three warp sticks in each direction.

Figure 7.—Complicated lattice twining employed upon baby baskets.

Figure 8.—Twining upon multiple warp used in border finishing.

Figure 9.—Starting knot in which warp sticks are first joined by twining and then crossed.

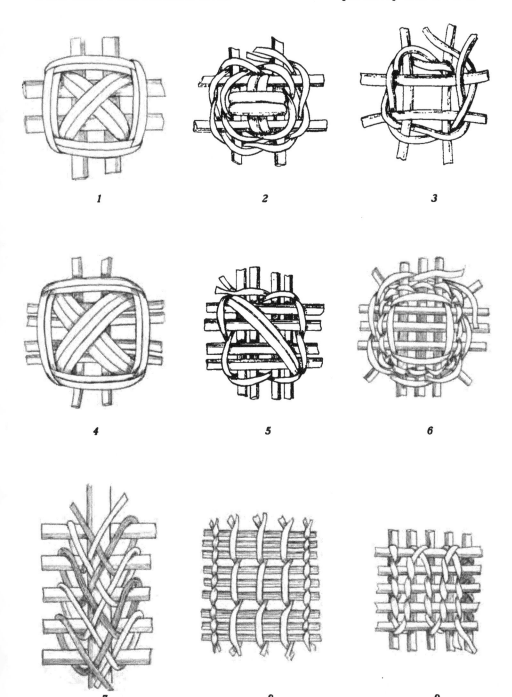

1　　　　　　2　　　　　　3

4　　　　　　5　　　　　　6

7　　　　　　8　　　　　　9

## EXPLANATION OF PLATE 16.

Figure 1.—Plain twined cooking basket. Horizontal arrangement of triangles with rhomboids. No. IVB 7302.*

Figure 2.—Diagonal twined, spheroidal basket. Diagonal arrangement of large triangles bordered by small ones with rhomboids in parallel rows between them. No. IVB 7269.

Figure 3.—Diagonal twined cooking basket approaching spheroidal form. Banded arrangement of diamond shaped designs. No. IVB 7280.

Figure 4.—Plain twined cooking basket. Small rhomboids crossed by a white line placed between horizontal rows of large triangles. No. IVB 7283.

Figure 5.—Diagonal twined cooking basket. Diagonally arranged triangles with rhomboids between. No. IVB 7286.

Figure 6.—Diagonal twined basket decorated with valley quail plumes and white shell beads. Triangles so arranged as to appear either diagonal and parallel, or diagonal and crossing. No. 1-366. × ¼.

---

* All numbers other than those of the series IV B refer to baskets in the Museum of the Department of Anthropology of the University of California; those of the series IV B refer to baskets in a collection made by the author and now the property of the Königliches Museum für Völkerkunde in Berlin.

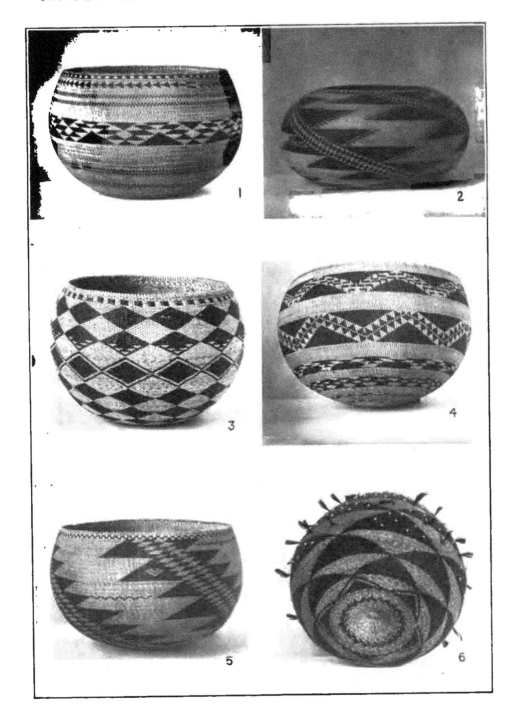

## EXPLANATION OF PLATE 17.

Figure 1.—Plain twined storage basket. Banded pattern composed of large triangles with rhomboids between. No. 1-3013. × $\frac{1}{12}$.

Figure 2.—Lattice-twined storage basket. Horizontally arranged triangles bordered by small ones. White shell beads are attached to the basket by means of the twining material itself. No. IVB 7270.

Figure 3.—Plain twined cooking basket. Banded arrangement of quail plume designs. The *dau* appears in the middle band. No. 1-367. × $\frac{1}{7}$.

Figure 4.—Lattice-twined storage basket of spherical form. The upper bands of triangles have white zigzags and the lower ones rhomboids. No. 1-3069. × $\frac{1}{8}$.

Figure 5.—Diagonal twined basket. Diagonally arranged triangles, rows of rhomboids between. No. 1-3030. × $\frac{1}{6}$.

Figure 6.—Diagonal twined cylindrical cooking basket. A crossing arrangement of triangles within triangles which enclose small rhomboids. No. 1-3022. × $\frac{1}{8}$.

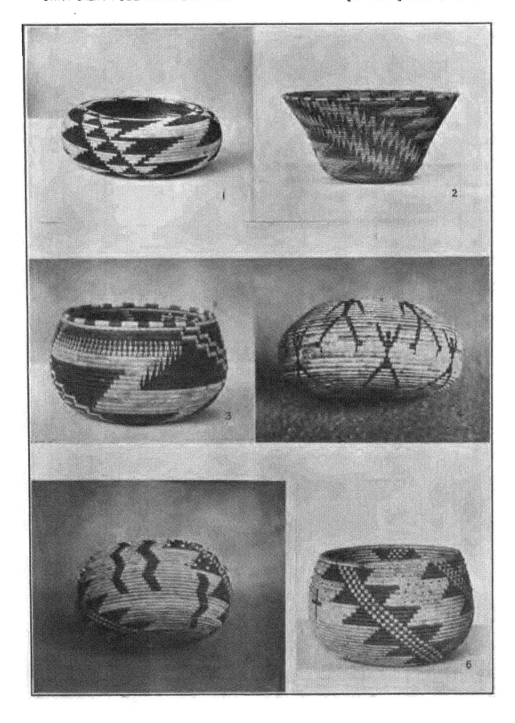

## EXPLANATION OF PLATE 19.

Figure 1.—Coiled on single-rod foundation, truncated-cone-shaped basket. Diagonally arranged double row of triangles with white rectangles between. An initial design is shown on the bottom. No. 1-3058. × ¼.

Figure 2.—Coiled, truncated-cone-shaped basket. Diagonal arrangement of triangles with a double row of zigzags between. No. 1-3012. × ⅒.

Figure 3.—Coiled, hemispherical basket. Crossing diagonal rows of triangles with rows of small rectangles. The human figure, a motive of late origin, is introduced. No. 1-3074. × ⅒.

Figure 4.—Coiled, elliptical basket decorated with red feathers of the woodpecker and groups of shell beads. Vertically placed pattern. No. IVB 7218.

Figure 5.—Coiled, elliptical basket with feathers and abalone shell pendants attached. Pattern vertically arranged. No. IVB 7217.

Figure 6.—Coiled, elliptical basket. A zigzag pattern diagonally placed. No. IVB 7224.

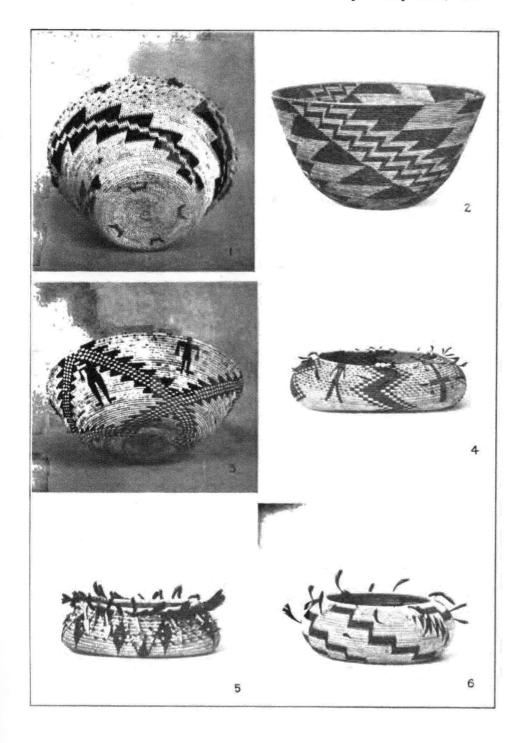

A ceremonial basket used by shamans for the storage of sacred objects. Coiled on single-rod foundation, elliptical in form with horizontally arranged patterns. No. 1-3009. × ⅛.

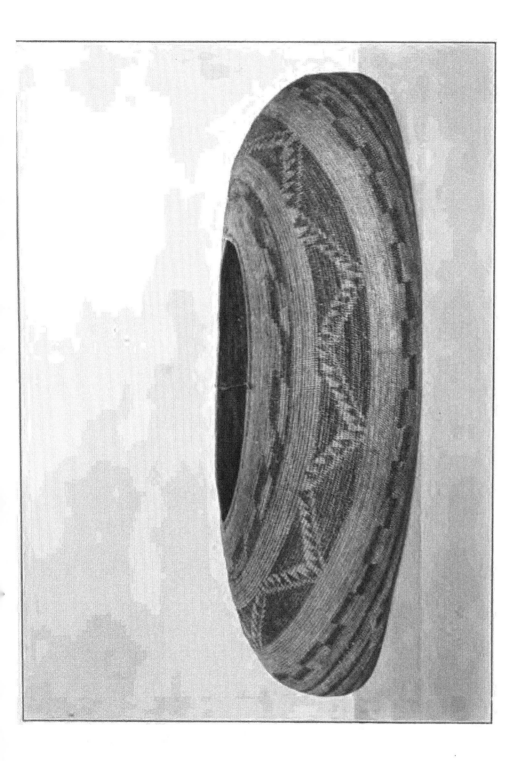

## EXPLANATION OF PLATE 21.

Figure 1.—Coiled basket completely covered with feathers which form designs. Triangular abalone pendants are attached. No. IVB 7212.

Figure 2.—Coiled basket with patterns worked in the feathers which entirely cover it. A bail and pendants of shell are added. The opening is provided with a row of quail plumes. No. IVB 7207.

Figure 3.—Coiled basket of single-rod foundation, elliptical in form. The horizontal bands are interrupted and rectangles arranged in a white triangle. No. IVB 7222.

Figure 4.—Coiled basket completely covered with variously colored feathers presenting the pattern. No. IVB 7209.

Figure 5.—Feather-covered, coiled basket. The opening has a continuous row of shell beads. No. IVB 7208.

Figure 6.—Coiled, elliptical basket decorated with feathers and beads. Crossing triangles extend over the bottom as well as the sides. No. IVB 1719.

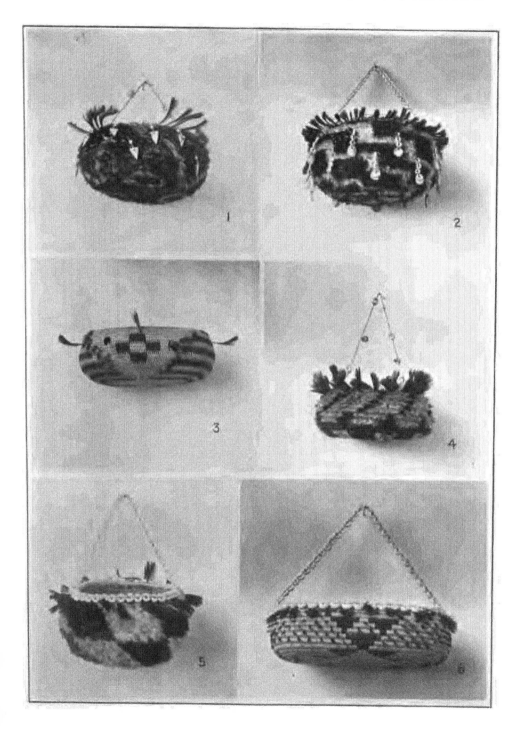

EXPLANATION OF PLATE 22.

Closely twined conical burden baskets.

Figure 1.—Diagonal twined with a hoop-bound opening. Diagonally arranged triangles with zigzags between. Small, bordering triangles appear. No. 1-3016. × $\frac{1}{10}$.

Figure 2.—Diagonal twined and hoop-bound. Triangles diagonally arranged with zigzags.

Figure 3.—Diagonal twined. Pattern of diagonally arranged triangles with a row of white rhomboids. No. IVB 7272.

Figure 4.—Diagonal twined. A border triangle so repeated as to appear in horizontal bands, diagonal parallel rows, or diagonal crossing rows. No. IVB 7271.

Figure 5.—Diagonal twined. Triangles, and rhomboids diagonally arranged. No. IVB 7274.

Figure 6.—Plain twined. Rectangles and zigzags arranged in horizontal bands. No. IVB 7273.

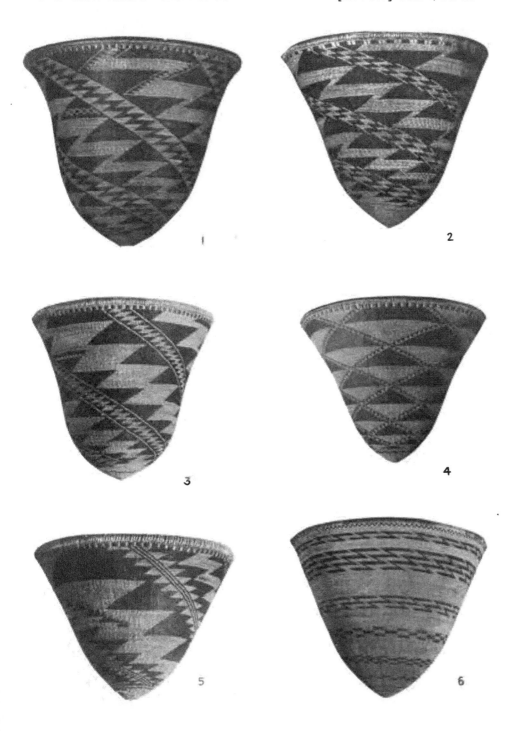

## EXPLANATION OF PLATE 23.

Figure 1.—Lattice-twined, plate-form, winnowing basket. Banded rows of triangles and rhomboids intentionally interrupted by a different design. No. IVB 7298.

Figure 2.—Lattice-twined, plate-form, winnowing basket. Horizontally arranged patterns. No. IVB 7295.

Figure 3.—Plain and lattice-twined mortar. The horizontal band of triangles with rhomboids between them show an interruption. No. IVB 7311.

Figure 4.—Plain and lattice-twined mortar in position. A hoop bound to the opening makes it rigid. Nos. 1-19, 1-2762, 1-3033. $\times \frac{1}{11}$.

Figure 5.—Plain and lattice-twined sifter provided with a string loop. Horizontal arrangement of rhomboids with an interruption. No. IVB 7305.

Figure 6.—Plain twined sifting basket with a peg for holding it. No. 1-10607. $\times \frac{1}{7}$.

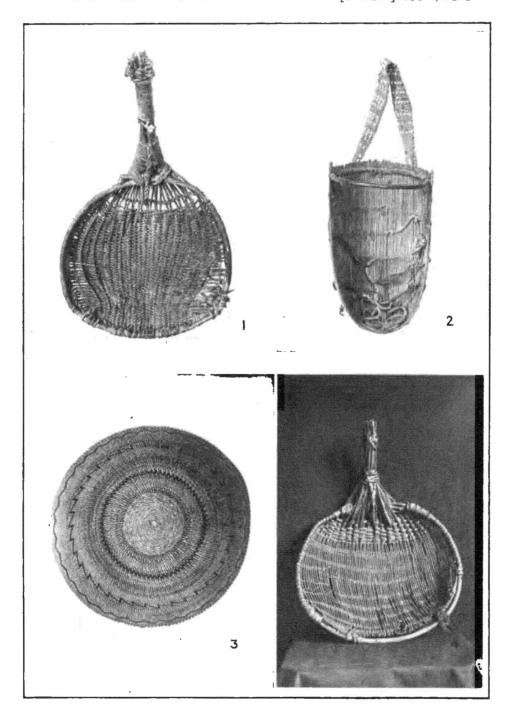

## EXPLANATION OF PLATE 25.

Figure 1.—Plain twined openwork basket. No. 1-450. × ⅛.

Figure 2.—Plain twined openwork storage basket decorated with beads. No. 1-4125. × ⅛.

Figure 3.—Lattice-twined, hemispherical basket. No. 1-4101. × ⅛.

Figure 4.—Plain twined on a multiple foundation. No. 1-4109. × ⅛.

Figure 5.—Plain twined openwork basket. No. 1-4110. × ⅛.

Figure 6.—Three-strand twined hemispherical openwork basket. No. 1-4470. × ⅛.

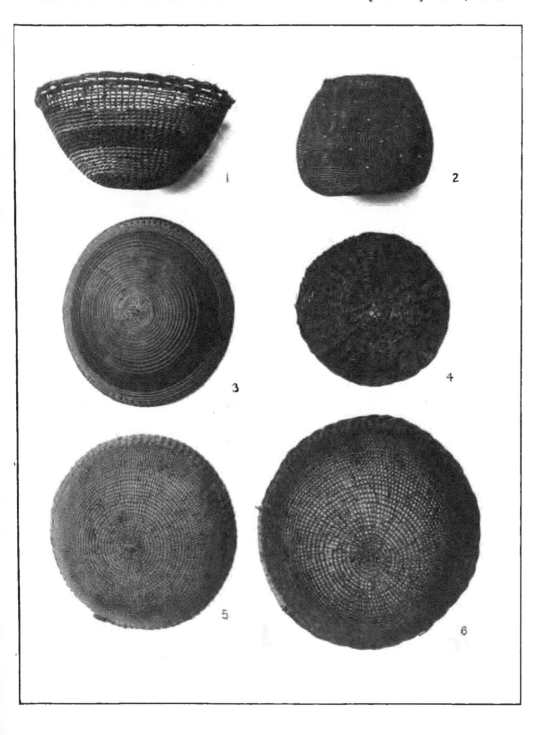

1

2

3

EXPLANATION OF PLATE 27.

Figure 1.—Openwork basket for catching woodpeckers.  No. 1-2607.  × 1/15.

Figure 2.—Long openwork basket set in a fish-wier as a trap.  No. 1-2581.
× 1/15.

Figure 3.—A fish-trap used in shallow water.  No. 1-2597.  × 1/15.

Figure 4.—A fish-trap used in connection with a wier.  No. 1-2605.  × 1/15.

Figure 5.—A trap used for catching fish in muddy water.  The hand is inserted in the opening above to remove the fish.  No. 1-2603.
× 1/15.

Figure 6.—A trap provided with a conical mouth to prevent the escape of the fish.  No. 1-2587.  × 1/15.

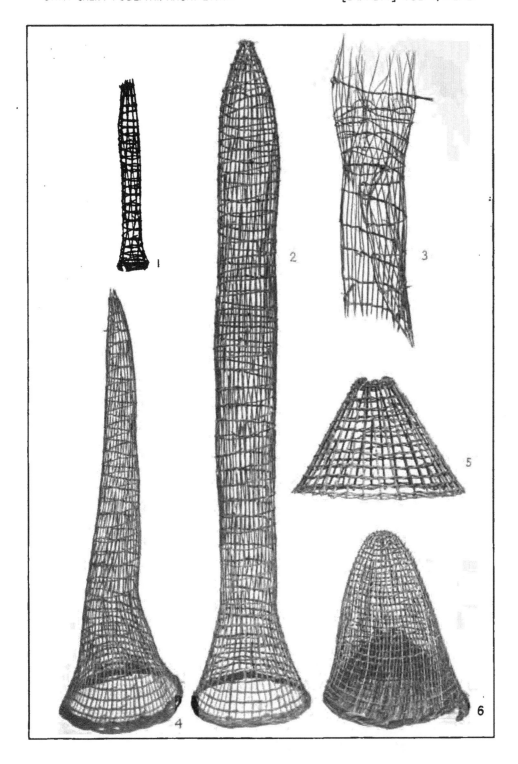

## EXPLANATION OF PLATE 28.

Figure 1.—A crossing pattern composed of double rows of triangles found on a closely twined burden basket. No. IVB 7279.

Figure 2.—A vertical arrangement of arrowhead designs. No. IVB 7226.

Figure 3.—Plain twined openwork quail trap. Nos. 1-2588, 1-2589, 1-2592, 1-2599.

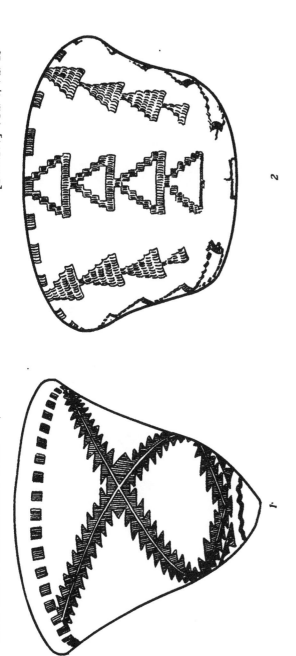

EXPLANATION OF PLATE 29.

Figures 1 to 4.—Four views of the same basket showing an individual or independent disposition of the designs. No. IVB 7241.

Figure 5.—Vertical arrangement of patterns. No. IVB 7259.

Figure 6.—An isolated design. No. IVB 7256.

1

2

3

4

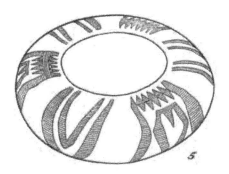

5

6

## EXPLANATION OF PLATE 30.

Figure 1.—Twined border.   No. 1-2604.

Figure 2.—Twined border having the appearance of braiding.   No. 1-3040.

Figure 3.—Border with warp sticks turned down and caught under the last round of twining.

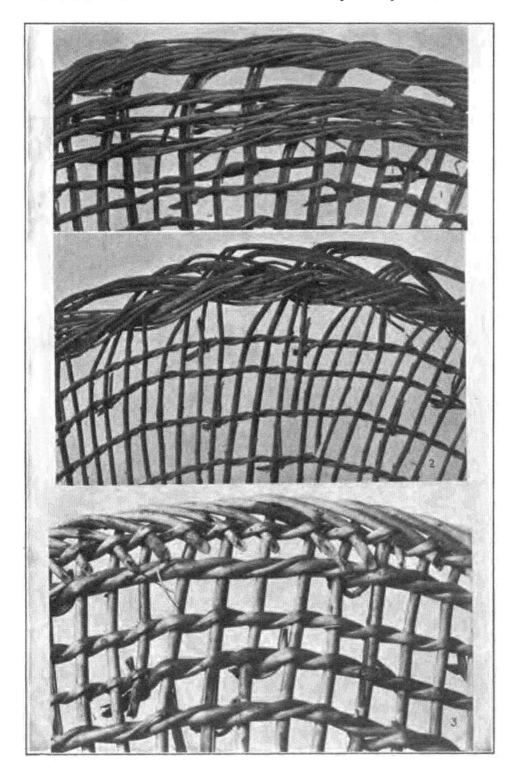

9 781166 170479